Be a cool calculator this summer with CGP!

Thirsty for summer Maths practice? This Daily Practice Book from CGP is more refreshing than an orange ice-lolly during a heatwave...

Inside, you'll find a page of Maths practice for every school day of the summer term, covering a huge range of skills from the Year 6 curriculum.

It's perfect for use in class or at home, with plenty of examples and some colourful fun to make sure pupils stay chilled!

What CGP is all about

Our sole aim here at CGP is to produce the highest quality books — carefully written, immaculately presented and dangerously close to being funny.

Then we work our socks off to get them out to you — at the cheapest possible prices.

Contents

☑ Use the tick boxes to help keep a record of which tests have been attempted.

Week 1
- ☑ Day 1 1
- ☑ Day 2 2
- ☑ Day 3 3
- ☑ Day 4 4
- ☑ Day 5 5

Week 2
- ☑ Day 1 6
- ☑ Day 2 7
- ☑ Day 3 8
- ☑ Day 4 9
- ☑ Day 5 10

Week 3
- ☑ Day 1 11
- ☑ Day 2 12
- ☑ Day 3 13
- ☑ Day 4 14
- ☑ Day 5 15

Week 4
- ☑ Day 1 16
- ☑ Day 2 17
- ☑ Day 3 18
- ☑ Day 4 19
- ☑ Day 5 20

Week 5
- ☑ Day 1 21
- ☑ Day 2 22
- ☑ Day 3 23
- ☑ Day 4 24
- ☑ Day 5 25

Week 6
- ☑ Day 1 26
- ☑ Day 2 27
- ☑ Day 3 28
- ☑ Day 4 29
- ☑ Day 5 30

Week 7
- ☑ Day 1 31
- ☑ Day 2 32
- ☑ Day 3 33
- ☑ Day 4 34
- ☑ Day 5 35

Week 8
- ☑ Day 1 36
- ☑ Day 2 37
- ☑ Day 3 38
- ☑ Day 4 39
- ☑ Day 5 40

Week 9

- [✓] Day 1 41
- [✓] Day 2 42
- [✓] Day 3 43
- [✓] Day 4 44
- [✓] Day 5 45

Week 10

- [✓] Day 1 46
- [✓] Day 2 47
- [✓] Day 3 48
- [✓] Day 4 49
- [✓] Day 5 50

Week 11

- [✓] Day 1 51
- [✓] Day 2 52
- [✓] Day 3 53
- [✓] Day 4 54
- [✓] Day 5 55

Week 12

- [✓] Day 1 56
- [✓] Day 2 57
- [✓] Day 3 58
- [✓] Day 4 59
- [✓] Day 5 60

Answers 61

Published by CGP

ISBN: 978 1 78908 660 7

Editors: Emily Garrett, Josie Gilbert, Rob Hayman, Duncan Lindsay, James Summersgill

With thanks to Sarah Pattison and Emma Wright for the proofreading.

With thanks to Lottie Edwards for the copyright research.

Clipart from Corel®

Printed by Bell & Bain Ltd, Glasgow.
Based on the classic CGP style created by Richard Parsons.

Text, design, layout and original illustrations© Coordination Group Publications Ltd. (CGP) 2020
All rights reserved.

Photocopying this book is not permitted, even if you have a CLA licence.
Extra copies are available from CGP with next day delivery • 0800 1712 712 • www.cgpbooks.co.uk

How to Use this Book

- This book contains 60 daily practice tests.

- We've split them into 12 sections — that's roughly one for each week of the Year 6 summer term.

- Each week is made up of 5 tests, so there's one for every school day of the term (Monday – Friday).

- Each test should take about 10 minutes to complete.

- The tests contain a mix of topics from Year 6 Maths. New Year 6 topics are gradually introduced through Weeks 1 to 3.

- The remaining weeks recap topics from throughout Year 6 Maths.

- Each test looks something like this:

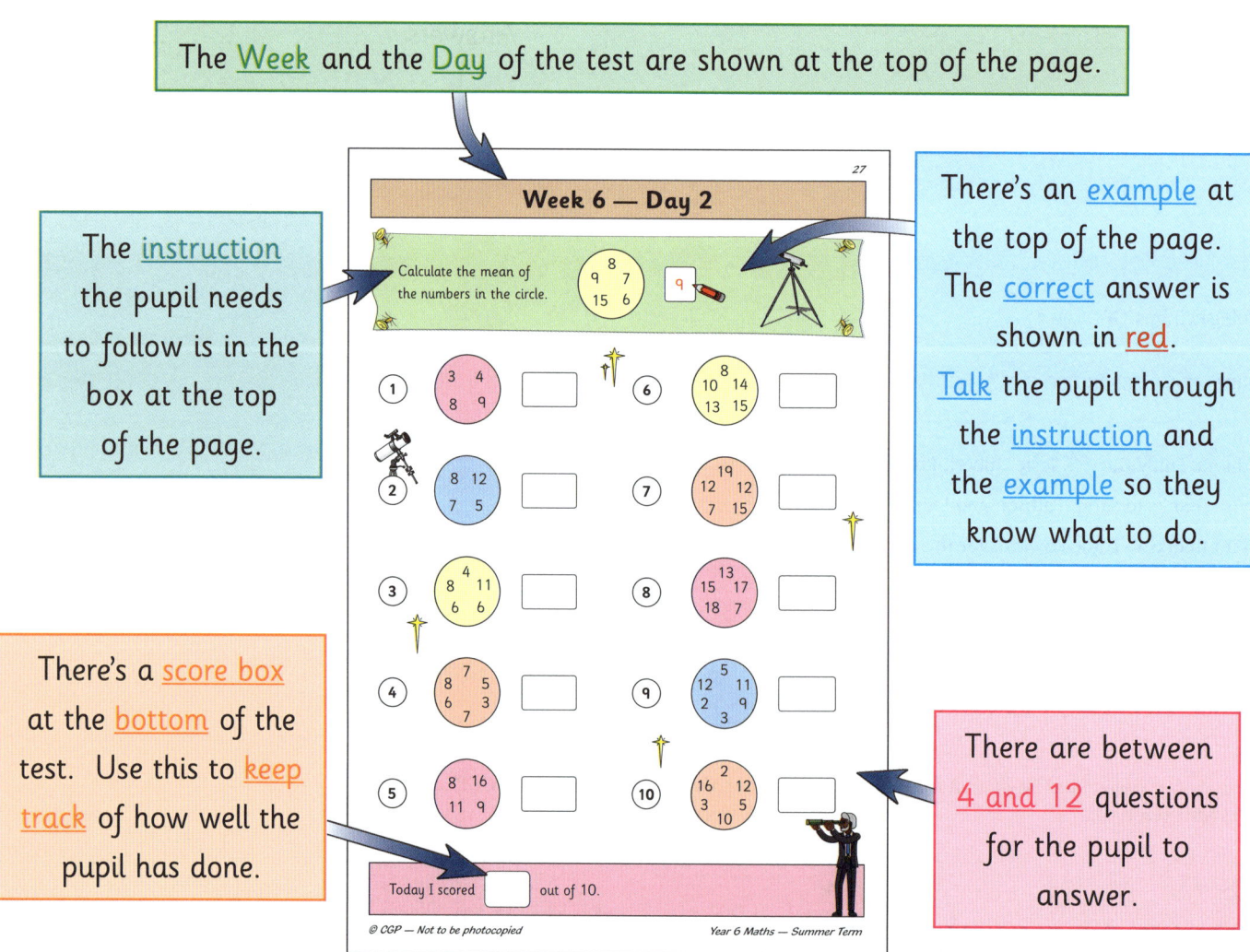

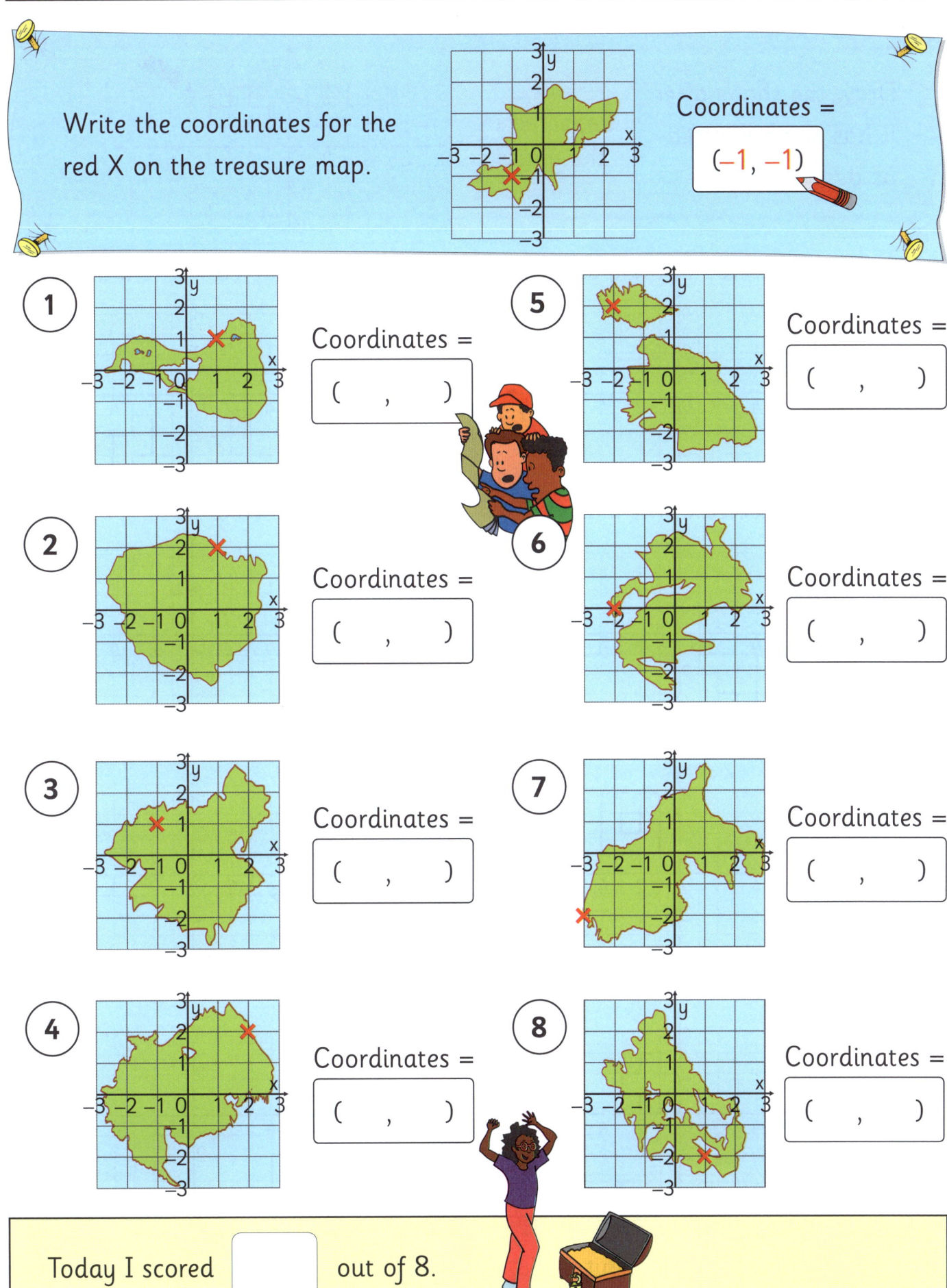

Week 1 — Day 2

Draw the shape after it has been reflected as described.

Reflected in the y-axis.

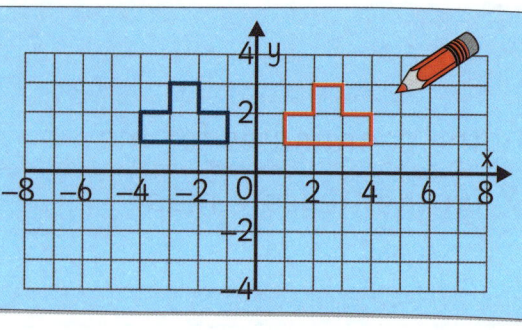

1. Reflected in the y-axis.

2. Reflected in the x-axis.

3. Reflected in the x-axis.

4. Reflected in the y-axis.

5. Reflected in the y-axis.

6. Reflected in the x-axis.

7. Reflected in the y-axis.

8. Reflected in the x-axis.

Today I scored ☐ out of 8.

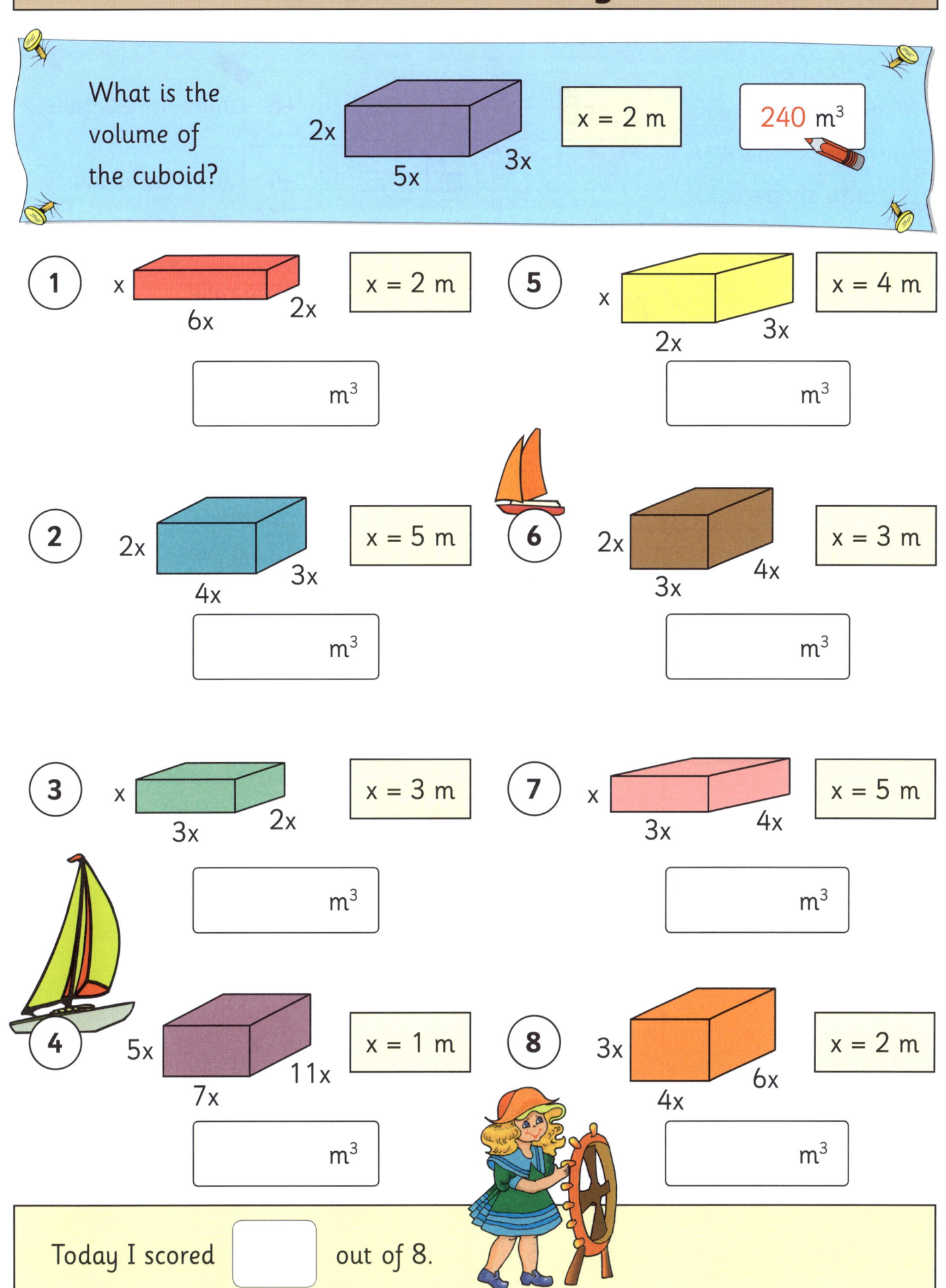

Week 1 — Day 4

Describe the translation that maps shape A onto shape B.

+8 units horizontally,
−4 units vertically.

1) ☐ units horizontally, ☐ units vertically.

2) ☐ units horizontally, ☐ units vertically.

3) ☐ units horizontally, ☐ units vertically.

4) ☐ units horizontally, ☐ units vertically.

5) ☐ units horizontally, ☐ units vertically.

Today I scored ☐ out of 5.

Week 1 — Day 5

Some items in a sports shop have had their prices reduced. Tick the item that has the biggest percentage discount.

Football: £25 to £5 ✓

Rugby ball: £10 to £3 ☐

1. Trainers: £100 to £52 ☐
Socks: £8 to £4 ☐

2. Swimsuit: £10 to £5 ☐
Snorkel: £20 to £12 ☐

3. Racket: £50 to £35 ☐
Balls: £5 to £4 ☐

4. Shorts: £10 to £6 ☐
Shirt: £30 to £21 ☐

5. Bat: £150 to £120 ☐
Balls: £20 to £15 ☐

6. Skis: £160 to £120 ☐
Goggles: £50 to £44 ☐

7. Bike: £200 to £150 ☐
Helmet: £60 to £48 ☐

8. Club: £320 to £240 ☐
Gloves: £40 to £34 ☐

9. Gloves: £72 to £18 ☐
Pads: £15 to £6 ☐

10. Boots: £75 to £39 ☐
Shin pads: £25 to £12 ☐

Today I scored ☐ out of 10.

Week 2 — Day 1

Write a calculation that you could do to estimate the answer.

(2.04 + 5.93) × 208 126

(2 + 6) × 200 000

1. (497 402 − 100 726) × 3.07

2. (7.11 + 4.02) × 19 764

3. (8045 + 3876) ÷ 4.08

4. 893 082 × (6.06 + 2.93)

5. (207 856 + 483 912) × 8.97

6. (583 904 + 904 872) ÷ 5.32

7. 2.12 × (314 632 + 601 516)

8. (389 239 − 208 752) ÷ 1.95

9. 713 184 ÷ (7.69 − 1.34)

10. 6.01 × (812 034 − 99 812)

Today I scored ☐ out of 10.

Week 2 — Day 2

Work out the mean of the numbers in the box.

| 6 | 11 | 8 | 13 | 12 |

10

1) | 8 | 5 | 6 | 9 |

2) | 12 | 9 | 5 | 10 |

3) | 6 | 2 | 4 | 6 | 7 |

4) | 16 | 7 | 14 | 11 |

5) | 10 | 7 | 12 | 6 | 5 |

6) | 15 | 7 | 8 | 5 | 16 | 3 |

7) | 9 | 13 | 8 | 10 | 15 |

8) | 15 | 7 | 18 | 3 | 2 |

9) | 8 | 14 | 13 | 7 | 14 | 16 |

10) | 11 | 15 | 4 | 9 | 13 | 14 |

Today I scored ☐ out of 10.

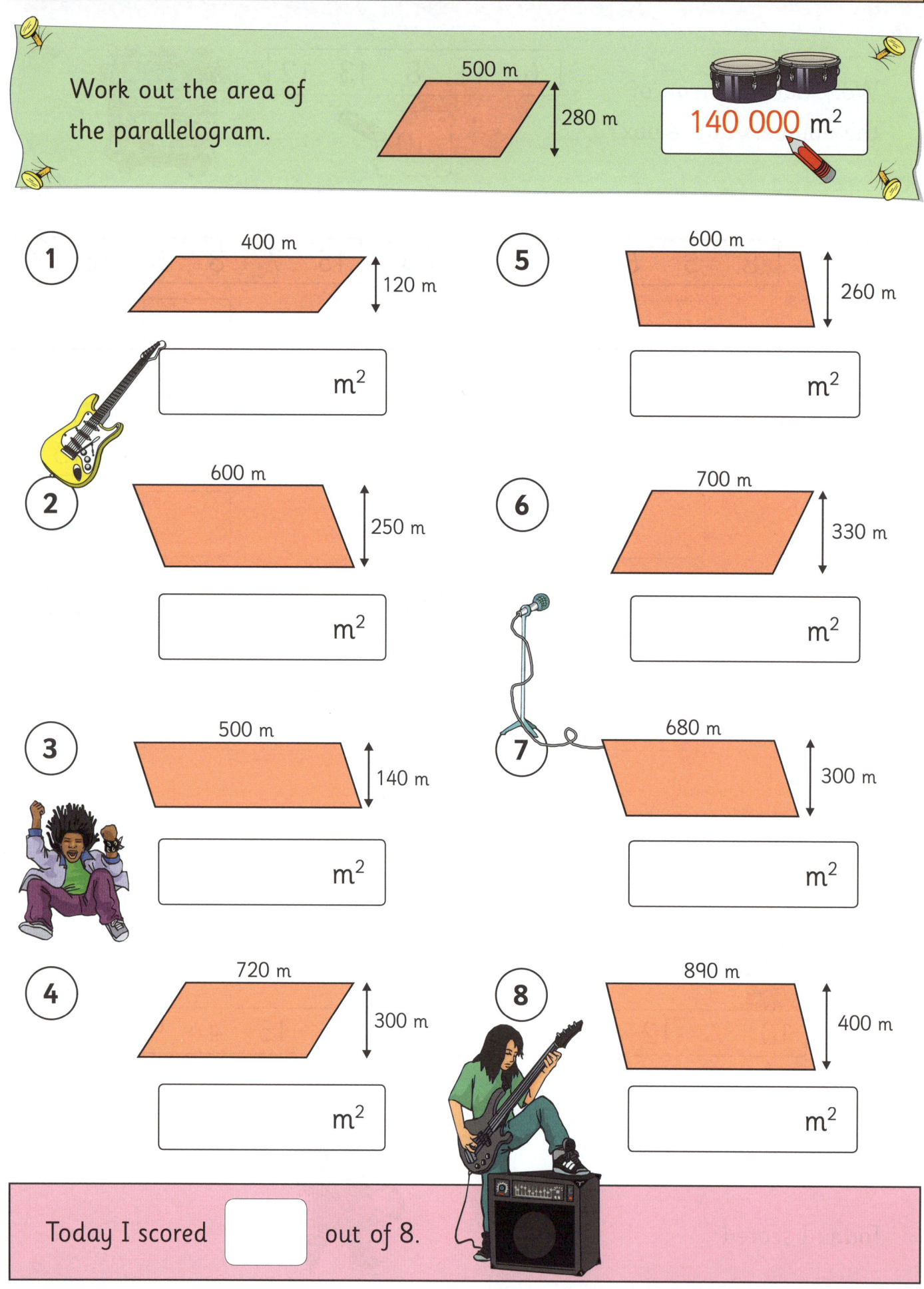

Week 2 — Day 4

The height of a plant was measured for 5 weeks. Draw the line graph for the data given in the table.

Week	1	2	3	4	5
Height (cm)	2	8	10	13	14

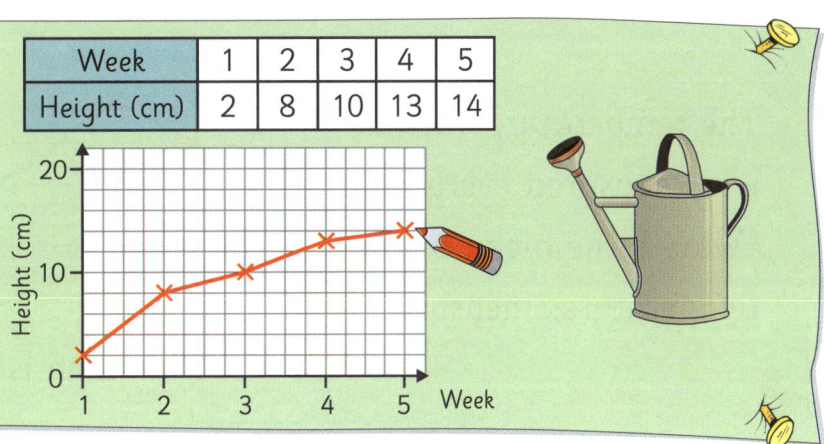

1

Week	1	2	3	4	5
Height (cm)	4	8	12	14	20

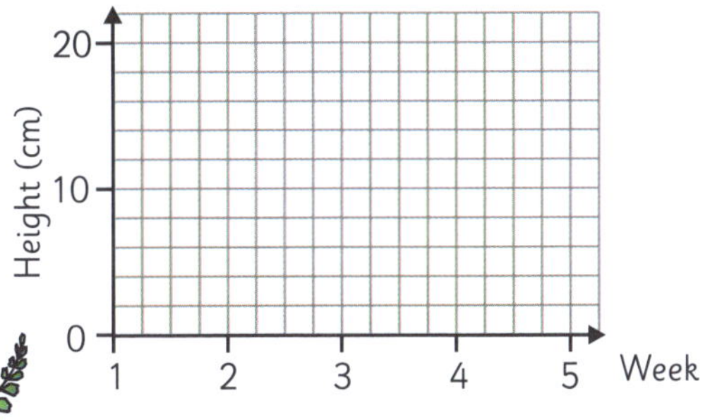

2

Week	1	2	3	4	5
Height (cm)	0	5	6	10	16

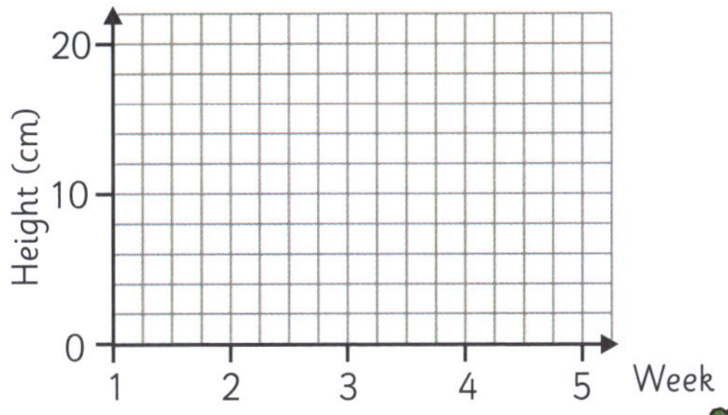

3

Week	1	2	3	4	5
Height (cm)	8	10	11	16	19

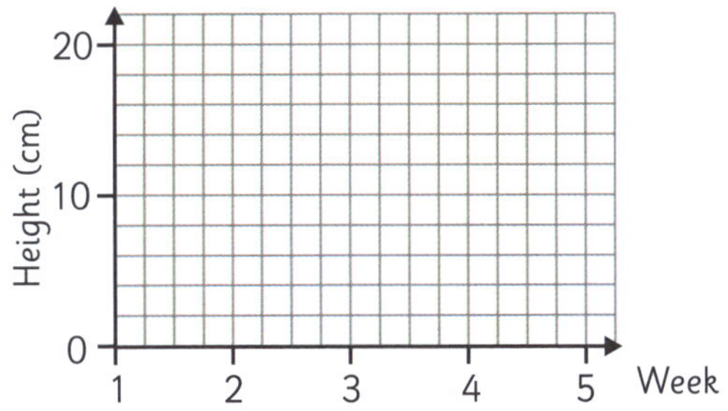

4

Week	1	2	3	4	5
Height (cm)	3	4	4	13	15

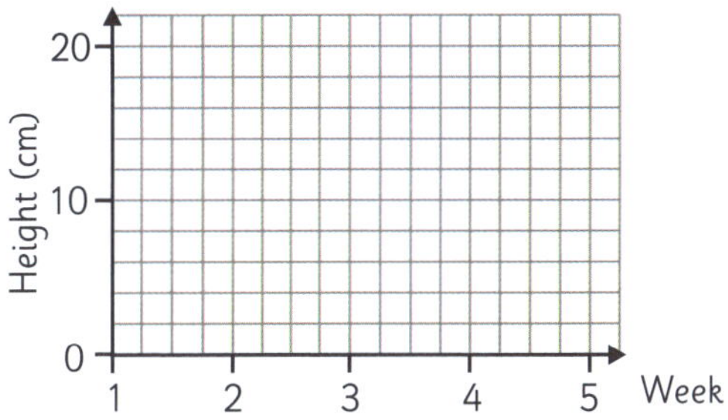

5

Week	1	2	3	4	5
Height (cm)	9	12	16	17	19

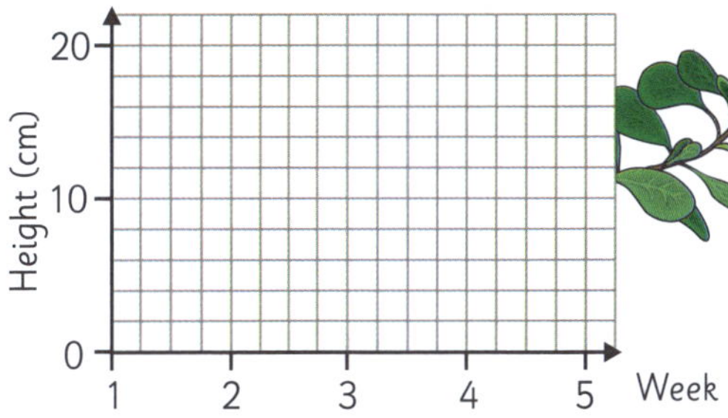

6

Week	1	2	3	4	5
Height (cm)	3	11	15	15	18

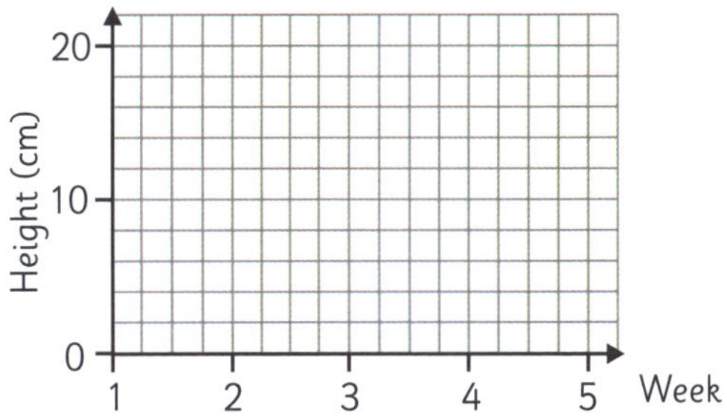

Today I scored ☐ out of 6.

Week 2 — Day 5

The temperature outside was measured every hour. What is the mean of the temperatures measured?

The mean is **5** °C.

1. The mean is ☐ °C.

2. The mean is ☐ °C.

3. The mean is ☐ °C.

4. The mean is ☐ °C.

5. The mean is ☐ °C.

6. The mean is ☐ °C.

Today I scored ☐ out of 6.

Week 3 — Day 1

Write the correct answer in its simplest form. $\frac{2}{5} \div 4 = \boxed{\frac{1}{10}}$

1) $\frac{1}{6} \div 4 =$

2) $\frac{3}{10} \div 5 =$

3) $\frac{3}{4} \div 7 =$

4) $\frac{1}{8} \div 5 =$

5) $\frac{5}{8} \div 10 =$

6) $\frac{2}{3} \div 8 =$

7) $\frac{7}{9} \div 7 =$

8) $\frac{8}{9} \div 6 =$

9) $\frac{6}{11} \div 4 =$

10) $\frac{4}{7} \div 8 =$

11) $\frac{3}{8} \div 9 =$

12) $\frac{6}{7} \div 12 =$

Today I scored ☐ out of 12.

Week 3 — Day 2

The table shows the number of people in an event. Complete the pie chart to show this information, using a protractor and ruler.

Event	Number	Angle
Skittles	13	130°
Ring toss	15	150°
Sprint	8	80°

1

Event	Number	Angle
Leap frog	5	90°
Sack race	10	180°
Relay race	5	90°

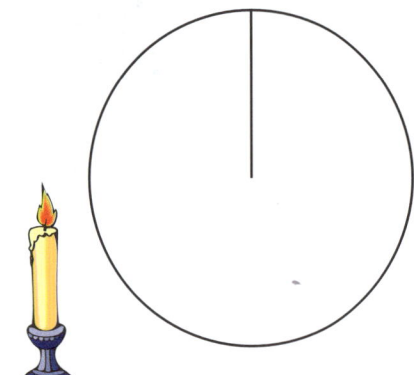

3

Event	Number	Angle
Hula hoop	11	110°
Sack race	10	100°
Leap frog	15	150°

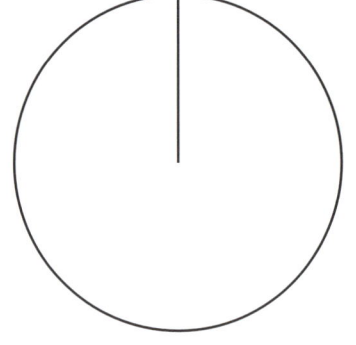

2

Event	Number	Angle
Tug of war	6	120°
Relay race	8	160°
Skittles	4	80°

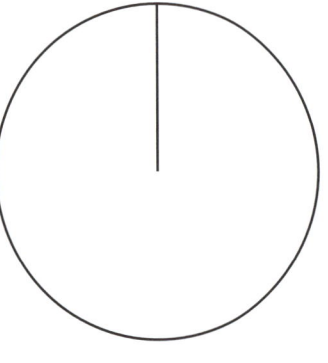

4

Event	Number	Angle
Coconut shy	25	125°
Tug of war	40	200°
Ring toss	7	35°

Today I scored ☐ out of 4.

Week 3 — Day 3

What is the total weight of the instruments in kg?

Saxophone: 2.2 kg
Flute: 450 g
Trombone: 1.32 kg

3.97 kg

1. Bagpipes: 2.61 kg
   Sitar: 3.12 kg
   Cello: 2.94 kg
   ☐ kg

2. Ukulele: 610 g
   Trumpet: 1.11 kg
   French horn: 2.56 kg
   ☐ kg

3. Accordion: 5.64 kg
   Piccolo: 161 g
   Keyboard: 5.22 kg
   ☐ kg

4. Piano: 261 kg
   Harp: 38 kg
   Oboe: 591 g
   ☐ kg

5. Guitar: 2.741 kg
   Mandolin: 1050 g
   Xylophone: 2301 g
   ☐ kg

6. Violin: 396 g
   Cymbals: 1894 g
   Bongos: 2.805 kg
   ☐ kg

7. Tuba: 12.8 kg
   Recorder: 164 g
   Bassoon: 3460 g
   ☐ kg

8. Triangle: 169 g
   Clarinet: 794 g
   Harmonica: 87 g
   ☐ kg

Today I scored ☐ out of 8.

Week 3 — Day 4

A box of tiles contains only green, purple and orange tiles. What percentage of the tiles are purple?

47% are green tiles.
$\frac{17}{50}$ are orange tiles.
19% are purple tiles.

1) 81% are green tiles.
$\frac{1}{10}$ are orange tiles.
☐ % are purple tiles.

2) 13% are green tiles.
$\frac{24}{50}$ are orange tiles.
☐ % are purple tiles.

3) 28% are green tiles.
$\frac{8}{25}$ are orange tiles.
☐ % are purple tiles.

4) 2% are green tiles.
$\frac{4}{5}$ are orange tiles.
☐ % are purple tiles.

5) 19% are green tiles.
$\frac{16}{20}$ are orange tiles.
☐ % are purple tiles.

6) 18% are green tiles.
$\frac{13}{20}$ are orange tiles.
☐ % are purple tiles.

7) 21% are green tiles.
$\frac{19}{25}$ are orange tiles.
☐ % are purple tiles.

8) 11% are green tiles.
$\frac{17}{20}$ are orange tiles.
☐ % are purple tiles.

Today I scored ☐ out of 8.

Week 3 — Day 5

The pie chart shows the proportion of different gems in a bag. Complete the sentence.

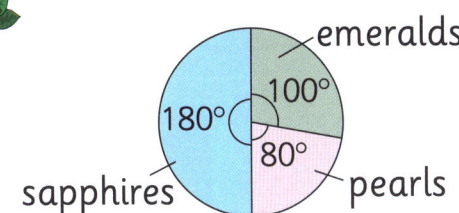

There are 36 gems in total. There are **6** rubies.

1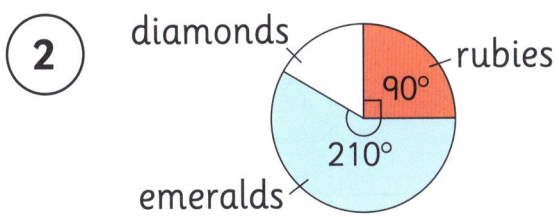

There are 36 gems in total.
There are ☐ sapphires.

4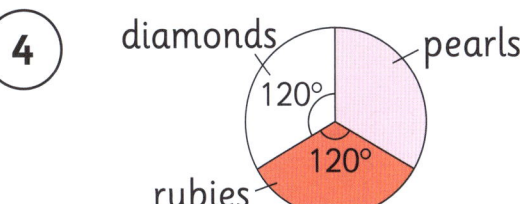

There are 12 gems in total.
There are ☐ pearls

2

diamonds, rubies 90°, emeralds 210°

There are 12 gems in total.
There are ☐ emeralds.

5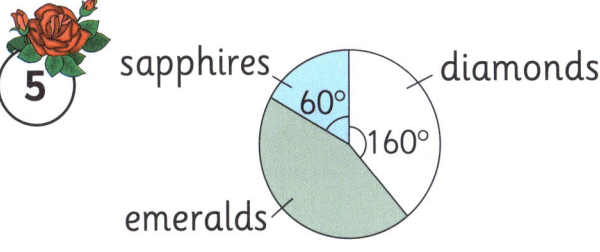

There are 18 gems in total.
There are ☐ emeralds.

3

opals 140°, sapphires, rubies

There are 36 gems in total.
There are ☐ opals.

6

opals 80°, sapphires 220°, pearls

There are 18 gems in total.
There are ☐ pearls.

Today I scored ☐ out of 6.

Week 4 — Day 1

What are the coordinates of point z on the rectangle?

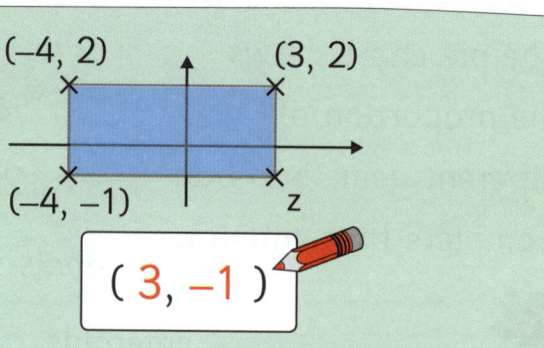

(3, –1)

1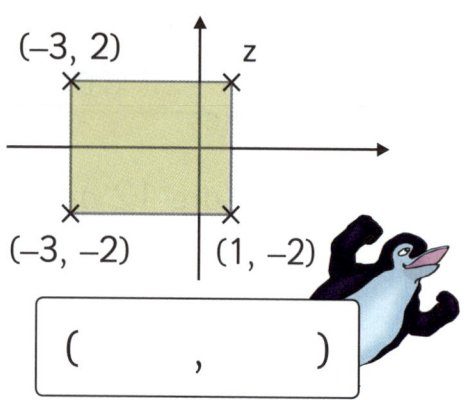

(,)

2

(–1, 3)   z

(–1, –2)   (2, –2)

(,)

3

(–4, 1)   (3, 1)

(–4, –3)   z

(,)

4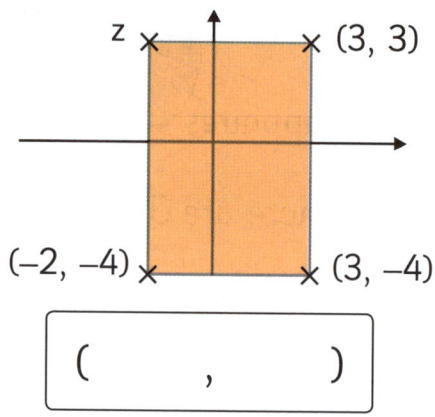

(,)

5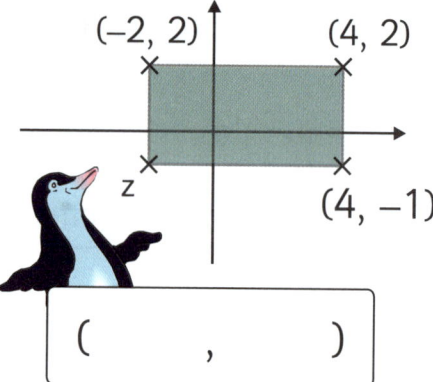

(,)

6

(–5, 2)   (2, 2)

z   (2, –3)

(,)

Today I scored ☐ out of 6.

Week 4 — Day 2

What fraction of the biscuits are chocolate cookies? Give your answer in its simplest form.

$\frac{3}{4}$ of the biscuits are cookies.
$\frac{2}{5}$ of the cookies are chocolate.
$\frac{3}{10}$ of the biscuits are chocolate cookies.

1) $\frac{5}{6}$ of the biscuits are cookies.
$\frac{1}{2}$ of the cookies are chocolate.
☐ of the biscuits are chocolate cookies.

2) $\frac{1}{4}$ of the biscuits are cookies.
$\frac{3}{7}$ of the cookies are chocolate.
☐ of the biscuits are chocolate cookies.

3) $\frac{7}{10}$ of the biscuits are cookies.
$\frac{4}{5}$ of the cookies are chocolate.
☐ of the biscuits are chocolate cookies.

4) $\frac{5}{8}$ of the biscuits are cookies.
$\frac{2}{3}$ of the cookies are chocolate.
☐ of the biscuits are chocolate cookies.

5) $\frac{7}{8}$ of the biscuits are cookies.
$\frac{3}{5}$ of the cookies are chocolate.
☐ of the biscuits are chocolate cookies.

6) $\frac{6}{11}$ of the biscuits are cookies.
$\frac{5}{6}$ of the cookies are chocolate.
☐ of the biscuits are chocolate cookies.

7) $\frac{3}{8}$ of the biscuits are cookies.
$\frac{6}{7}$ of the cookies are chocolate.
☐ of the biscuits are chocolate cookies.

8) $\frac{5}{12}$ of the biscuits are cookies.
$\frac{8}{9}$ of the cookies are chocolate.
☐ of the biscuits are chocolate cookies.

Today I scored ☐ out of 8.

Week 4 — Day 3

Every week Abby spends 6 hours at the gym and goes to three classes. How many minutes does she spend in class 3?

Class	Time
1	1 hour 27 minutes
2	95 minutes
3	178 minutes

1.

Class	Time
1	1 hour 20 minutes
2	150 minutes
3	minutes

2.

Class	Time
1	125 minutes
2	2 hours 30 minutes
3	minutes

3.

Class	Time
1	1 hour 3 minutes
2	135 minutes
3	minutes

4.

Class	Time
1	2 hours 17 minutes
2	82 minutes
3	minutes

5.

Class	Time
1	134 minutes
2	2 hours 36 minutes
3	minutes

6.

Class	Time
1	1 hour 18 minutes
2	164 minutes
3	minutes

7.

Class	Time
1	114 minutes
2	1 hour 53 minutes
3	minutes

8.

Class	Time
1	149 minutes
2	1 hour 27 minutes
3	minutes

Today I scored [ ] out of 8.

Week 4 — Day 4

Write the missing fraction in its simplest form. $1\frac{2}{5} + \boxed{\frac{3}{4}} = 2\frac{3}{20}$

1) $3\frac{1}{4} + \boxed{} = 3\frac{7}{12}$

6) $2\frac{5}{7} + \boxed{} = 3\frac{3}{14}$

2) $2\frac{1}{2} + \boxed{} = 2\frac{9}{10}$

7) $2\frac{1}{3} + \boxed{} = 3\frac{5}{24}$

3) $4\frac{3}{5} + \boxed{} = 4\frac{23}{30}$

8) $3\frac{3}{8} + \boxed{} = 4\frac{7}{40}$

4) $1\frac{2}{3} + \boxed{} = 2\frac{1}{6}$

9) $1\frac{4}{7} + \boxed{} = 2\frac{5}{21}$

5) $1\frac{5}{6} + \boxed{} = 2\frac{14}{24}$

10) $2\frac{3}{4} + \boxed{} = 3\frac{5}{28}$

Today I scored $\boxed{}$ out of 10.

Week 4 — Day 5

What is the area of the rectangle after it has been enlarged?

2 m, 3 m — Enlarged by scale factor 3. **54 m²**

1) 4 m, 7 m — Enlarged by scale factor 2. ___ m²

2) 2 m, 5 m — Enlarged by scale factor 3. ___ m²

3) 3 m, 8 m — Enlarged by scale factor 5. ___ m²

4) 5 m, 10 m — Enlarged by scale factor 3. ___ m²

5) 3 m, 6 m — Enlarged by scale factor 4. ___ m²

6) 4 m, 6 m — Enlarged by scale factor 6. ___ m²

7) 3 m, 7 m — Enlarged by scale factor 8. ___ m²

8) 4 m, 8 m — Enlarged by scale factor 7. ___ m²

Today I scored ___ out of 8.

Week 5 — Day 1

Complete the sentence. The 5 in the number 3 250 184 has the value **50 000**

1. The 3 in the number 628 311 has the value

2. The 7 in the number 571 098 has the value

3. The 4 in the number 422 235 has the value

4. The 1 in the number 6 784 319 has the value

5. The 8 in the number 8 766 005 has the value

6. The 9 in the number 8 907 613 has the value

7. The 6 in the number 4 113 687 has the value

8. The 1 in the number 1 234 598 has the value

9. The 5 in the number 9 254 618 has the value

10. The 4 in the number 6 064 108 has the value

11. The 2 in the number 5 280 751 has the value

12. The 7 in the number 9 679 423 has the value

Today I scored ☐ out of 12.

Week 5 — Day 2

Complete the number sentence.   1640 g = **1.64** kg

1) 2400 g = ☐ kg

2) 6450 g = ☐ kg

3) ☐ g = 5.76 kg

4) ☐ g = 0.81 kg

5) 7684 g = ☐ kg

6) ☐ g = 0.466 kg

7) ☐ g = 8.061 kg

8) ☐ g = 9.073 kg

9) 846 g = ☐ kg

10) ☐ g = 0.055 kg

11) 23 g = ☐ kg

12) 7 g = ☐ kg

Today I scored ☐ out of 12.

Week 5 — Day 3

Use a protractor and ruler to draw the isosceles triangle being described. It has two 3 cm sides with a 25° angle between them.

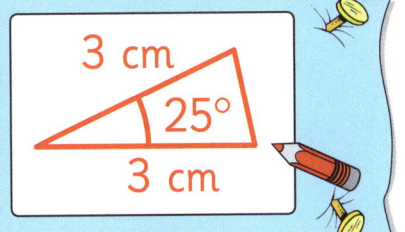

1. It has two 4 cm sides with a 30° angle between them.

2. It has two 2 cm sides with a 50° angle between them.

3. It has two 5 cm sides with a 20° angle between them.

4. It has two 3 cm sides with a 15° angle between them.

5. It has two 4 cm sides with a 25° angle between them.

6. It has two 5 cm sides with a 5° angle between them.

Today I scored ☐ out of 6.

Week 5 — Day 4

Work out how far the person has travelled.

Martin has travelled 85% of 6000 m.

5100 m

1. Joey has travelled 20% of 8000 m.
   ☐ m

2. Letitia has travelled 60% of 4000 m.
   ☐ m

3. Hans has travelled 90% of 3000 m.
   ☐ m

4. Ahmed has travelled 15% of 6000 m.
   ☐ m

5. Zola has travelled 45% of 7000 m.
   ☐ m

6. Rosa has travelled 65% of 9000 m.
   ☐ m

7. Polly has travelled 11% of 2000 m.
   ☐ m

8. Kiran has travelled 34% of 5000 m.
   ☐ m

9. Yvonne has travelled 48% of 8000 m.
   ☐ m

10. Jeff has travelled 79% of 9000 m.
    ☐ m

Today I scored ☐ out of 10.

Week 5 — Day 5

A number of toys are shared equally between some shops. How many toys are left over?

1361 toys are shared between 15 shops.
11 toys are left over.

1. 1458 toys are shared between 12 shops.
☐ toys are left over.

2. 2378 toys are shared between 11 shops.
☐ toys are left over.

3. 3318 toys are shared between 15 shops.
☐ toys are left over.

4. 7894 toys are shared between 20 shops.
☐ toys are left over.

5. 1738 toys are shared between 21 shops.
☐ toys are left over.

6. 2871 toys are shared between 16 shops.
☐ toys are left over.

7. 5613 toys are shared between 14 shops.
☐ toys are left over.

8. 4788 toys are shared between 23 shops.
☐ toys are left over.

Today I scored ☐ out of 8.

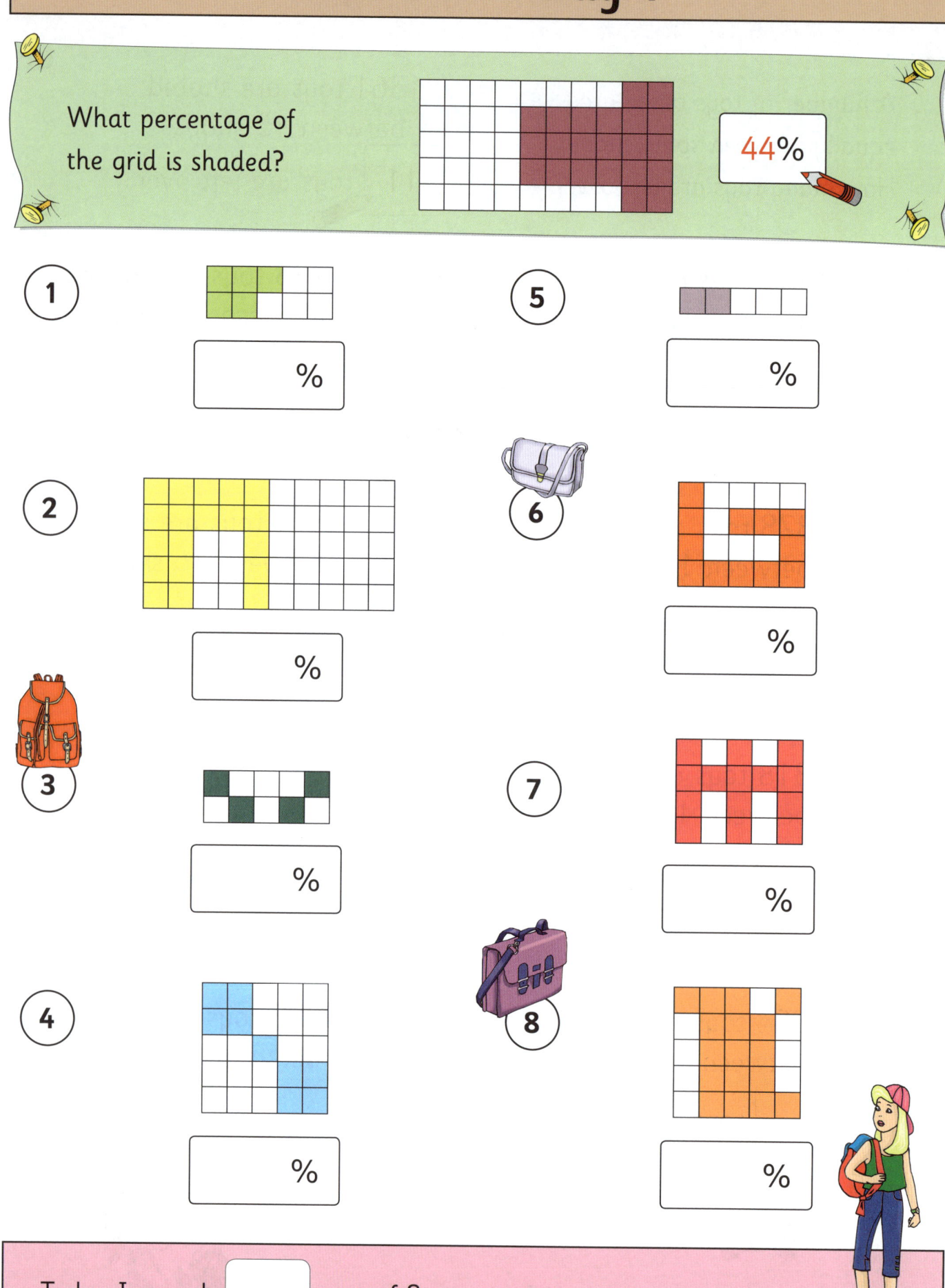

Week 6 — Day 2

Calculate the mean of the numbers in the circle. [example shows 8, 9, 7, 15, 6 → 9]

1) 3, 4, 8, 9
2) 8, 12, 7, 5
3) 4, 8, 11, 6, 6
4) 7, 8, 5, 6, 3, 7
5) 8, 16, 11, 9
6) 8, 10, 14, 13, 15
7) 19, 12, 12, 7, 15
8) 13, 15, 17, 18, 7
9) 5, 12, 11, 2, 9, 3
10) 2, 16, 12, 3, 5, 10

Today I scored ☐ out of 10.

Week 6 — Day 3

Look at the formula for the number sequence. Use the formula to complete the sentence.

6n + 7

The 20th term is 127

① 4n + 1
The 7th term is ☐

② 3n + 7
The 20th term is ☐

③ 2n − 4
The 24th term is ☐

④ 6n − 5
The 10th term is ☐

⑤ 7n + 11
The 8th term is ☐

⑥ 3n + 20
The 15th term is ☐

⑦ 8n − 15
The 50th term is ☐

⑧ 9n − 12
The 100th term is ☐

⑨ 7n + 18
The 12th term is ☐

⑩ 12n − 16
The 9th term is ☐

⑪ 11n − 22
The 12th term is ☐

⑫ 12n − 27
The 8th term is ☐

Today I scored ☐ out of 12.

Week 6 — Day 4

How far has the person got left to run in km?

Sarah has run 250 m of a 3 km race. She still has 2.75 km left to run.

1. Brandy has run 160 m of a 4 km race. She still has ___ km left to run.

2. Christoff has run 240 m of a 6 km race. He still has ___ km left to run.

3. Daniel has run 681 m of a 2 km race. He still has ___ km left to run.

4. Iman has run 2161 m of an 8 km race. She still has ___ km left to run.

5. Hayley has run 1488 m of a 6 km race. She still has ___ km left to run.

6. Phillip has run 1277 m of a 7 km race. He still has ___ km left to run.

7. Grace has run 2904 m of a 9 km race. She still has ___ km left to run.

8. Sverre has run 3049 m of an 11 km race. He still has ___ km left to run.

9. Jamal has run 2086 m of a 15 km race. He still has ___ km left to run.

10. Josefina has run 6017 m of a 10 km race. She still has ___ km left to run.

Today I scored ___ out of 10.

Week 6 — Day 5

Draw a circle around the division that is equal to the fraction.

$\frac{21}{28}$ — (3 ÷ 4) / 10 ÷ 14 / 28 ÷ 21

1) $\frac{6}{19}$ — 19 ÷ 6 / 1 ÷ 3 / 6 ÷ 19

5) $\frac{8}{42}$ — 2 ÷ 21 / 4 ÷ 22 / 4 ÷ 21

2) $\frac{24}{26}$ — 13 ÷ 12 / 12 ÷ 13 / 5 ÷ 6

6) $1\frac{8}{9}$ — 8 ÷ 9 / 17 ÷ 9 / 5 ÷ 3

3) $\frac{18}{24}$ — 9 ÷ 8 / 9 ÷ 12 / 9 ÷ 10

7) $2\frac{2}{6}$ — 7 ÷ 3 / 6 ÷ 14 / 2 ÷ 1

4) $\frac{12}{30}$ — 6 ÷ 15 / 3 ÷ 10 / 12 ÷ 6

8) $2\frac{10}{12}$ — 24 ÷ 12 / 18 ÷ 2 / 17 ÷ 6

Today I scored [ ] out of 8.

Week 7 — Day 1

What is the total weight in kilograms?

A 3.216 kg bag and a 2360 g bag.

5.576 kg

1. A 1.37 kg bag and a 3520 g bag.
   ___ kg

2. A 2.442 kg bag and a 457 g bag.
   ___ kg

3. A 4.62 kg bag and a 3298 g bag.
   ___ kg

4. A 3.865 kg bag and a 1330 g bag.
   ___ kg

5. A 3.726 kg bag and a 571 g bag.
   ___ kg

6. A 2.451 kg bag and a 4903 g bag.
   ___ kg

7. A 1.604 kg bag and a 3489 g bag.
   ___ kg

8. A 2.934 kg bag and a 587 g bag.
   ___ kg

9. A 4.782 kg bag and a 674 g bag.
   ___ kg

10. A 5.928 kg bag and a 96 g bag.
    ___ kg

Today I scored ___ out of 10.

Week 7 — Day 2

How far has the person driven in kilometres?

Milo has driven 40 miles.

64 km

1. Toby has driven 10 miles. ___ km
2. Cora has driven 20 miles. ___ km
3. Phoebe has driven 15 miles. ___ km
4. Jakob has driven 30 miles. ___ km
5. Bevan has driven 50 miles. ___ km
6. Hari has driven 25 miles. ___ km
7. Gabby has driven 35 miles. ___ km
8. Eden has driven 45 miles. ___ km
9. Omar has driven 55 miles. ___ km
10. Nadia has driven 60 miles. ___ km

Today I scored ___ out of 10.

Week 7 — Day 3

The letters in the equation stand for whole numbers bigger than 0. List all the possible pairs of values of X and Y.

$(X + 2) \times Y = 14$

X = 5   Y = 2

X = 12   Y = 1

1 $(X + 1) \times Y = 8$

X =   Y =

X =   Y =

X =   Y =

2 $(X + 3) \times Y = 12$

X =   Y =

X =   Y =

X =   Y =

3 $(X + 1) \times Y = 10$

X =   Y =

X =   Y =

X =   Y =

4 $(X + 4) \times Y = 20$

X =   Y =

X =   Y =

X =   Y =

5 $(X + 2) \times Y = 15$

X =   Y =

X =   Y =

X =   Y =

6 $(X + 6) \times Y = 24$

X =   Y =

X =   Y =

X =   Y =

Today I scored ☐ out of 6.

Week 7 — Day 4

Find the size of the largest share.

360 is split in the ratio 4:5 → 200

1) 120 is split in the ratio 1:5

2) 200 is split in the ratio 3:7

3) 240 is split in the ratio 1:2

4) 150 is split in the ratio 2:3

5) 280 is split in the ratio 1:3

6) 350 is split in the ratio 3:4

7) 440 is split in the ratio 4:7

8) 180 is split in the ratio 2:7

9) 540 is split in the ratio 1:5

10) 450 is split in the ratio 1:4

11) 420 is split in the ratio 2:5

12) 560 is split in the ratio 3:5

Today I scored ☐ out of 12.

Week 7 — Day 5

The two cuboids described have the same volume. Fill in the length of the missing side.

Cuboid A has sides of 4 cm, 5 cm and 3 cm.

Cuboid B has sides of 5 cm, 2 cm and 6 cm.

1 Cuboid C has sides of 3 cm, 8 cm and 3 cm.

Cuboid D has sides of 6 cm, 3 cm and ___ cm.

2 Cuboid E has sides of 2 cm, 12 cm and 4 cm.

Cuboid F has sides of 4 cm, 3 cm and ___ cm.

3 Cuboid G has sides of 5 cm, 9 cm and 8 cm.

Cuboid H has sides of 3 cm, 10 cm and ___ cm.

4 Cuboid J has sides of 8 cm, 11 cm and 6 cm.

Cuboid K has sides of 12 cm, 4 cm and ___ cm.

5 Cuboid L has sides of 16 cm, 6 cm and 5 cm.

Cuboid M has sides of 10 cm, 4 cm and ___ cm.

6 Cuboid N has sides of 9 cm, 8 cm and 14 cm.

Cuboid P has sides of 8 cm, 7 cm and ___ cm.

Today I scored ___ out of 6.

Week 8 — Day 1

Write the number in words.   1 465 096   One million, four hundred and sixty five thousand and ninety six

1) 234 875

2) 132 011

3) 908 766

4) 2 344 781

5) 4 567 890

6) 7 067 802

7) 6 008 041

Today I scored ☐ out of 7.

Week 8 — Day 2

Complete the sentence.

For every 2 parties Glenn goes to, Caley goes to 3 parties. In total, they went to 25 parties last year. Caley went to **15** parties last year.

1. For every 3 parties Salim goes to, Cecilia goes to 1 party. In total, they went to 16 parties last year. Cecilia went to ☐ parties last year.

2. For every 5 parties Malika goes to, Lara goes to 1 party. In total, they went to 42 parties last year. Lara went to ☐ parties last year.

3. For every 3 parties Conor goes to, Dhavit goes to 4 parties. In total, they went to 35 parties last year. Conor went to ☐ parties last year.

4. For every 5 parties Haruko goes to, John goes to 3 parties. In total, they went to 56 parties last year. Haruko went to ☐ parties last year.

5. For every 5 parties Owain goes to, Hugh goes to 4 parties. In total, they went to 54 parties last year. Hugh went to ☐ parties last year.

6. For every 7 parties Jenny goes to, Honey goes to 5 parties. In total, they went to 84 parties last year. Jenny went to ☐ parties last year.

Today I scored ☐ out of 6.

Week 8 — Day 3

Both shapes have the same perimeter. Work out the area of the parallelogram.

3 cm, 10 cm (rectangle); 4 cm, 3 cm (parallelogram) → **27** cm²

1) Rectangle 4 cm × 8 cm; Parallelogram 5 cm, 3 cm → ☐ cm²

2) Rectangle 10 cm × 12 cm; Parallelogram 14 cm, 10 cm → ☐ cm²

3) Rectangle 2 cm × 16 cm; Parallelogram 13 cm, 9 cm → ☐ cm²

4) Rectangle 4 cm × 7 cm; Parallelogram 3 cm, 2 cm → ☐ cm²

5) Rectangle 5 cm × 17 cm; Parallelogram 10 cm, 9 cm → ☐ cm²

6) Rectangle 4 cm × 14 cm; Parallelogram 7 cm, 6 cm → ☐ cm²

Today I scored ☐ out of 6.

Week 8 — Day 4

The pie chart shows the proportion of stripy, spotty and plain socks in a pack of socks. The number of socks in a pack is shown. How many plain socks are there?

A pack of 36 socks.

15 plain socks

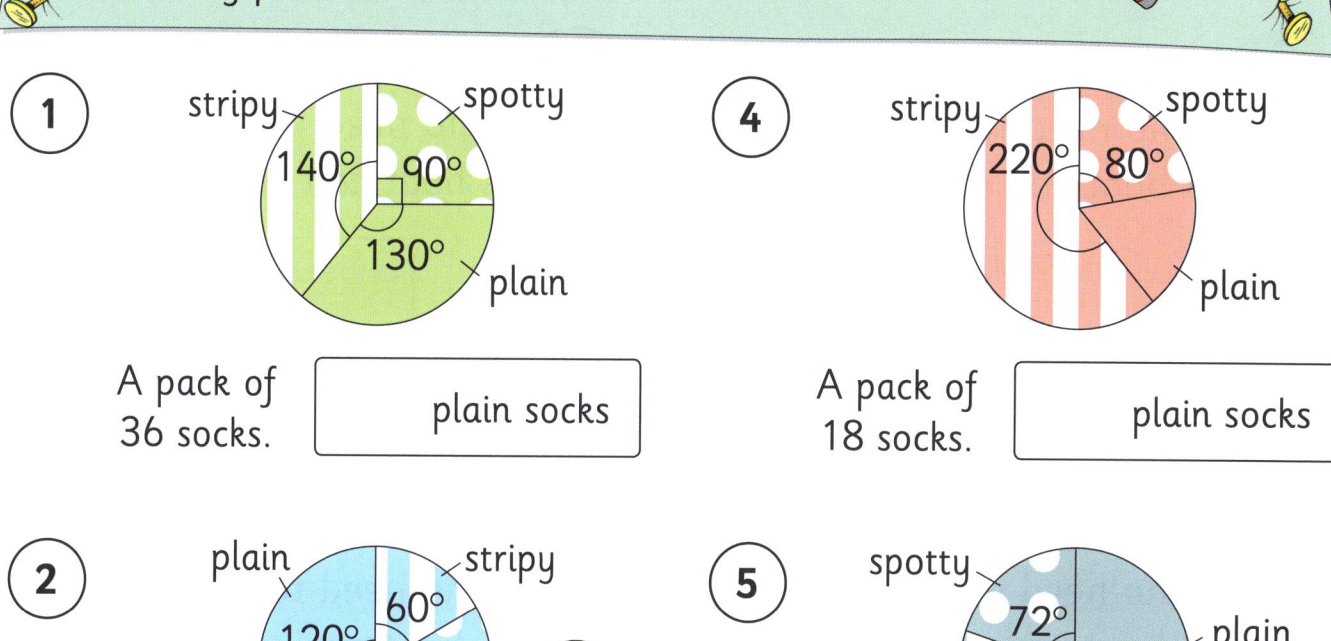

1) A pack of 36 socks. ☐ plain socks

4) A pack of 18 socks. ☐ plain socks

2) A pack of 12 socks. ☐ plain socks

5) A pack of 10 socks. ☐ plain socks

3) A pack of 36 socks. ☐ plain socks

6) A pack of 24 socks. ☐ plain socks

Today I scored ☐ out of 6.

Week 8 — Day 5

How many boats are needed to carry everyone across the lake?

There are 2516 people who need to cross the lake. A boat can carry 24 people.

105 boats

1. There are 1764 people who need to cross the lake. A boat can carry 15 people.

   ☐ boats

2. There are 2760 people who need to cross the lake. A boat can carry 21 people.

   ☐ boats

3. There are 2198 people who need to cross the lake. A boat can carry 18 people.

   ☐ boats

4. There are 8894 people who need to cross the lake. A boat can carry 44 people.

   ☐ boats

5. There are 6451 people who need to cross the lake. A boat can carry 29 people.

   ☐ boats

6. There are 5407 people who need to cross the lake. A boat can carry 38 people.

   ☐ boats

Today I scored ☐ out of 6.

Week 9 — Day 1

Find the difference in the temperatures of the two cities.

Wellington: −2 °C.
London: 21 °C.

23 °C

1. Minsk: −10 °C.
   Phoenix: 20 °C.   °C

6. Winnipeg: −22 °C.
   Taipei: 27 °C.   °C

2. Riga: −15 °C.
   Kingston: 25 °C.   °C

7. Singapore: 34 °C.
   Ottawa: −13 °C.   °C

3. Lima: 32 °C.
   Stockholm: −14 °C.   °C

8. Harbin: −23 °C.
   Nairobi: 28 °C.   °C

4. Dubai: 39 °C.
   Nuuk: −7 °C.   °C

9. Los Angeles: 29 °C.
   Oslo: −12 °C.   °C

5. Havana: 37 °C.
   Dublin: −6 °C.   °C

10. Helsinki: −19 °C.
    Bangkok: 33 °C.   °C

Today I scored ☐ out of 10.

Week 9 — Day 2

Write an equation for the rule given. If you take a number b, add 5 and divide it by 2, you get 10.

$(b + 5) \div 2 = 10$

1. If you take a number d, subtract 4 and multiply it by 2, you get 4.

2. If you take a number c, add 7 and multiply it by 4, you get 32.

3. If you take a number z, multiply it by 3 and add 5, you get 18.

4. If you take a number t, multiply it by 3 and divide it by 2, you get 6.

5. If you take a number x, divide it by 4 and subtract 2, you get 14.

6. If you take a number y, multiply it by 7 and divide it by 6, you get 22.

7. If you take a number q, subtract 17 and divide it by 11, you get 1.

8. If you take a number m, divide it by 9 and add 15, you get 36.

Today I scored ☐ out of 8.

Week 9 — Day 3

Draw the shape after it has been reflected as described.

Reflected in the y-axis.

1. Reflected in the x-axis.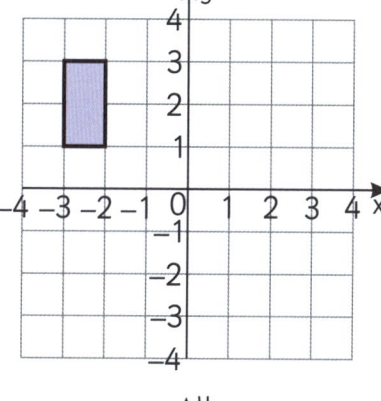

2. Reflected in the y-axis.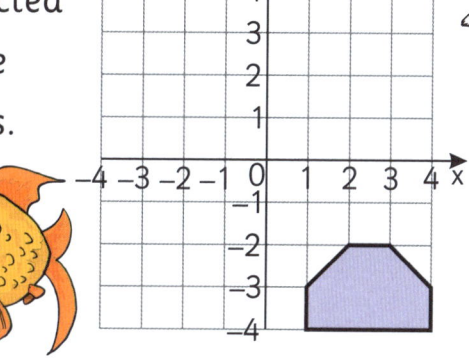

3. Reflected in the x-axis.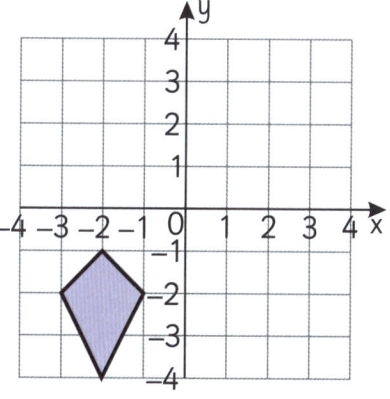

4. Reflected in the y-axis.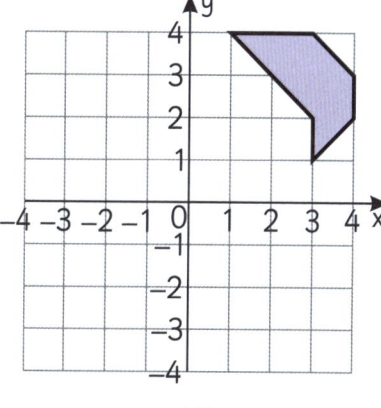

5. Reflected in the x-axis.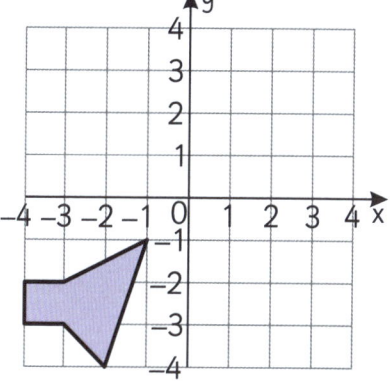

6. Reflected in the y-axis.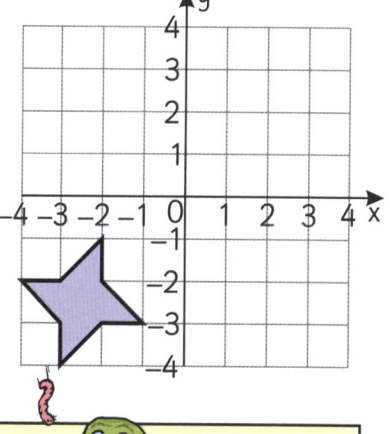

Today I scored ☐ out of 6.

Week 9 — Day 4

Who drank the most water? Clarisse drank $1\frac{5}{12}$ l, Arjen drank $1\frac{1}{6}$ l and Alexis drank $\frac{7}{4}$ l. **Alexis**

1 Natasha drank $1\frac{1}{3}$ l, Jess drank $1\frac{2}{9}$ l and Rick drank $\frac{23}{18}$ l.

4 Eric drank $2\frac{5}{9}$ l, Jasmine drank $\frac{8}{3}$ l and Miguel drank $2\frac{7}{15}$ l.

2 Summer drank $\frac{8}{7}$ l, Ryan drank $1\frac{1}{14}$ l and Sanjay drank $\frac{23}{21}$ l.

5 Kris drank $2\frac{3}{28}$ l, Adam drank $\frac{23}{8}$ l and Maria drank $2\frac{6}{7}$ l.

3 Felix drank $1\frac{3}{10}$ l, Claire drank $1\frac{2}{5}$ l and Haya drank $\frac{41}{30}$ l.

6 Akira drank $3\frac{1}{6}$ l, Zoe drank $3\frac{1}{8}$ l and Chloe drank $\frac{29}{9}$ l.

Today I scored ☐ out of 6.

Week 9 — Day 5

Two different items make up an outfit. By working out the price of each individual item, work out how many full outfits the person can buy.

Three shirts cost £60.
Five pairs of trousers cost £80.
Reggie has £180.

He can buy [5] full outfits.

1. Three jackets cost £600.
Four pairs of trousers cost £200.
Sonya has £500.

She can buy [ ] full outfits.

2. Eight jumpers cost £560.
Twelve skirts cost £480.
Isabelle has £330.

She can buy [ ] full outfits.

3. Six t-shirts cost £72.
Four pairs of shorts cost £100.
Terry has £370.

She can buy [ ] full outfits.

4. Seven shirts cost £210.
Nine kilts cost £540.
Angus has £360.

He can buy [ ] full outfits.

5. Six polo shirts cost £54.
Ten pairs of shorts cost £110.
Johan has £220.

He can buy [ ] full outfits.

6. Four blouses cost £180.
Eleven skirts cost £440.
Rabiya has £935.

She can buy [ ] full outfits.

7. Five t-shirts cost £40.
Eight pairs of jeans cost £160.
Edgar has £336.

He can buy [ ] full outfits.

8. Twelve jumpers cost £480.
Five pairs of leggings cost £60.
Judy has £676.

She can buy [ ] full outfits.

Today I scored [ ] out of 8.

Week 10 — Day 1

Use the area to find the length of the side labelled x on the parallelogram.

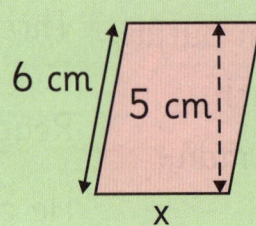

Area = 20 cm²

x = 4 cm

① 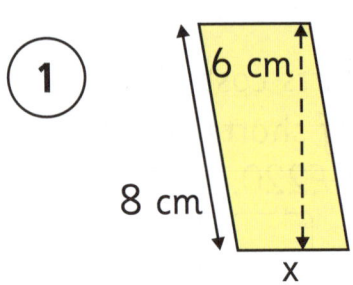 Area = 18 cm² x = ☐ cm

⑤ 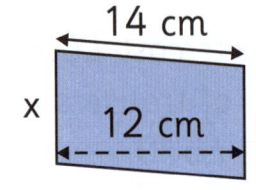 Area = 84 cm² x = ☐ cm

② 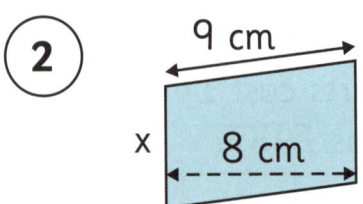 Area = 40 cm² x = ☐ cm

⑥ 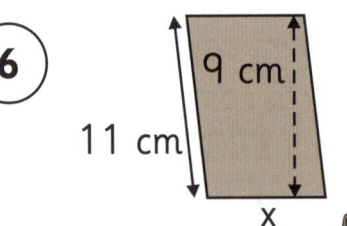 Area = 54 cm² x = ☐ cm

③ 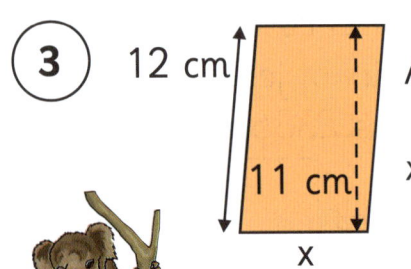 Area = 66 cm² x = ☐ cm

⑦ 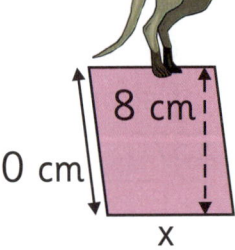 Area = 56 cm² x = ☐ cm

④ 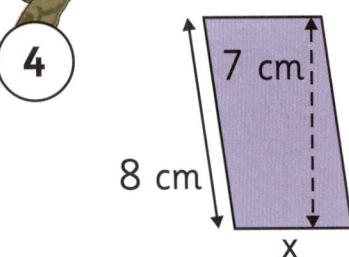 Area = 28 cm² x = ☐ cm

⑧ 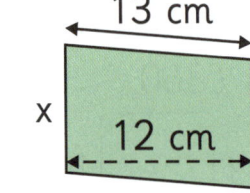 Area = 96 cm² x = ☐ cm

Today I scored ☐ out of 8.

Week 10 — Day 2

What is the sum of the interior angles of the regular polygon?

The polygon has 9 sides and an exterior angle of 40°.

1260°

1 The polygon has 6 sides and an exterior angle of 60°.

____°

2 The polygon has 10 sides and an exterior angle of 36°.

____°

3 The polygon has 5 sides and an exterior angle of 72°.

____°

4 The polygon has 12 sides and an exterior angle of 30°.

____°

5 The polygon has 20 sides and an exterior angle of 18°.

____°

6 The polygon has 30 sides and an exterior angle of 12°.

____°

7 The polygon has 18 sides and an exterior angle of 20°.

____°

8 The polygon has 24 sides and an exterior angle of 15°.

____°

Today I scored ____ out of 8.

Week 10 — Day 3

Circle the formula that gives the largest value of y.

When x = 5

$y = 2x + 7$ $y = 4x \div 2$ **(y = 3 + 3x)** ⬅ circled

1) When x = 7 $y = 9 + x$ $y = 2x + 3$ $y = 3x - 3$

2) When x = 3 $y = 4x \div 6$ $y = 3x - 5$ $y = 2 + x$

3) When x = 6 $y = x \div 3 + 6$ $y = 2x - 8$ $y = 9 - x \div 2$

4) When x = 10 $y = 3x - 7$ $y = 2x + 6$ $y = x + 12$

5) When x = 9 $y = x - 2$ $y = x \div 3 + 5$ $y = 2x \div 3$

6) When x = 8 $y = x + 3$ $y = 2x - 1$ $y = 4 + x \div 2$

7) When x = 4 $y = x \div 4 + 8$ $y = 4x - 6$ $y = 2x + 4$

8) When x = 12 $y = 2x \div 3$ $y = 3x \div 6$ $y = x \div 2 + 1$

Today I scored ☐ out of 8.

Week 10 — Day 4

How many centimetres of thread are used?

Bea uses 50 cm of thread to sew on 2 patches. How much thread does she use to sew on 6 patches?

150 cm

1 Debra uses 80 cm of thread to sew on 4 patches. How much thread does she use to sew on 8 patches?

_____ cm

2 Abe uses 60 cm of thread to sew on 5 patches. How much thread does he use to sew on 15 patches?

_____ cm

3 Carl uses 100 cm of thread to sew on 8 patches. How much thread does he use to sew on 2 patches?

_____ cm

4 Sue uses 125 cm of thread to sew on 3 patches. How much thread does she use to sew on 6 patches?

_____ cm

5 Toby uses 120 cm of thread to sew on 9 patches. How much thread does he use to sew on 3 patches?

_____ cm

6 Helga uses 145 cm of thread to sew on 7 patches. How much thread does she use to sew on 14 patches?

_____ cm

7 Flo uses 55 cm of thread to sew on 4 patches. How much thread does she use to sew on 16 patches?

_____ cm

8 Deion uses 180 cm of thread to sew on 12 patches. How much thread does he use to sew on 2 patches?

_____ cm

Today I scored _____ out of 8.

Week 10 — Day 5

How many grams of flour does the person have left?

A pie recipe uses 365 g of flour. Beth starts with 6000 g of flour and makes 7 pies.

3445 g

1) A pie recipe uses 242 g of flour. Charlie starts with 3000 g of flour and makes 4 pies.
☐ g

2) A pie recipe uses 196 g of flour. Felipe starts with 4000 g of flour and makes 5 pies.
☐ g

3) A pie recipe uses 317 g of flour. Esther starts with 6000 g of flour and makes 7 pies.
☐ g

4) A pie recipe uses 264 g of flour. Daryl starts with 5000 g of flour and makes 8 pies.
☐ g

5) A pie recipe uses 328 g of flour. Gale starts with 5000 g of flour and makes 7 pies.
☐ g

6) A pie recipe uses 281 g of flour. Kareem starts with 6000 g of flour and makes 6 pies.
☐ g

7) A pie recipe uses 279 g of flour. Ingrid starts with 7000 g of flour and makes 8 pies.
☐ g

8) A pie recipe uses 392 g of flour. Hana starts with 8000 g of flour and makes 9 pies.
☐ g

Today I scored ☐ out of 8.

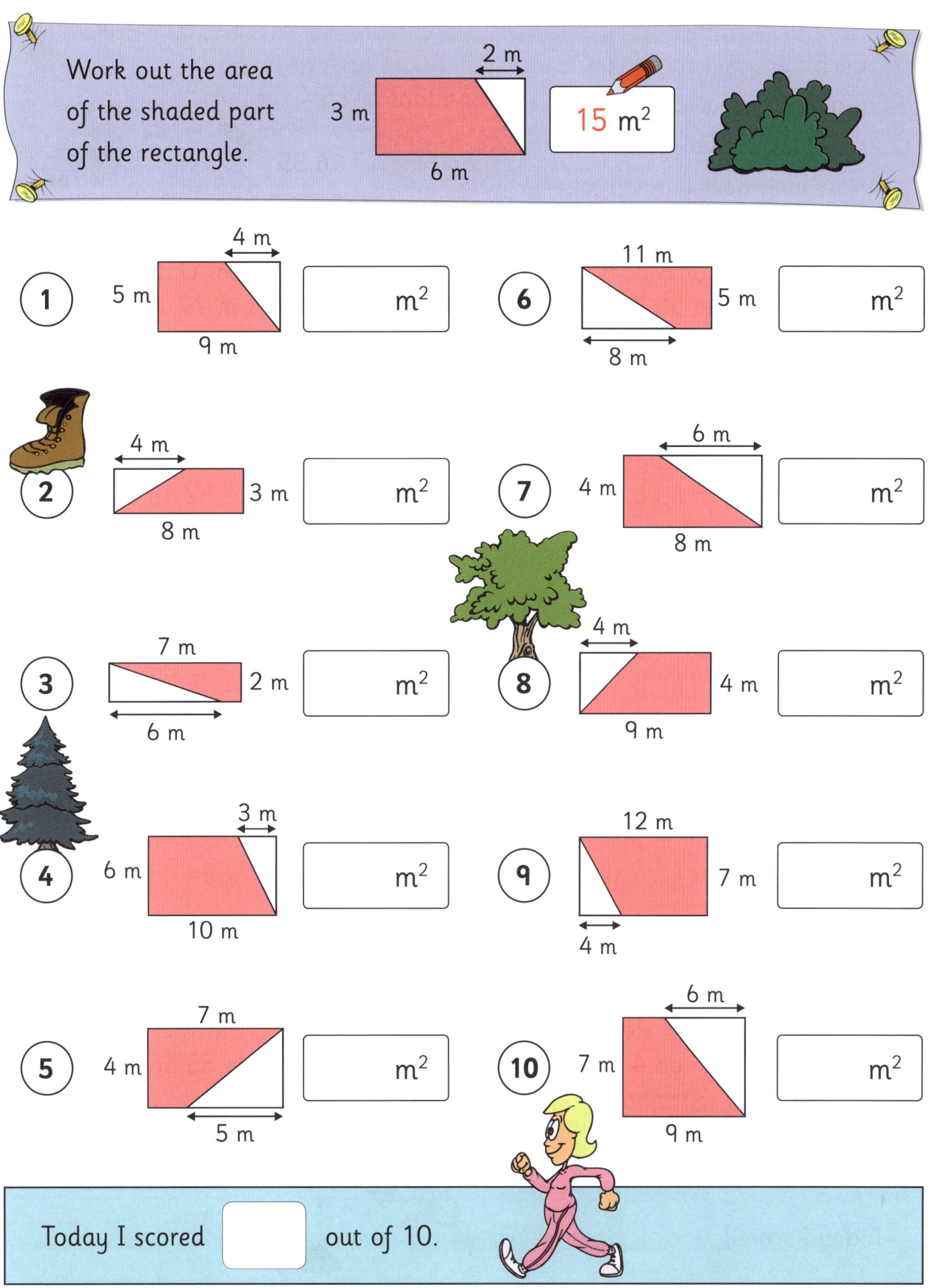

Week 11 — Day 2

Each lap a toy car makes around a circuit takes the same amount of time. How long does one lap take?

Car A does 4 laps in 65.4 seconds.

1 lap takes 16.35 seconds.

1. Car B does 5 laps in 56.3 seconds.
   1 lap takes ☐ seconds.

2. Car C does 8 laps in 63.6 seconds.
   1 lap takes ☐ seconds.

3. Car D does 6 laps in 52.5 seconds.
   1 lap takes ☐ seconds.

4. Car E does 4 laps in 42.6 seconds.
   1 lap takes ☐ seconds.

5. Car F does 5 laps in 68.4 seconds.
   1 lap takes ☐ seconds.

6. Car G does 6 laps in 77.1 seconds.
   1 lap takes ☐ seconds.

7. Car H does 9 laps in 92.43 seconds.
   1 lap takes ☐ seconds.

8. Car I does 5 laps in 85.75 seconds.
   1 lap takes ☐ seconds.

9. Car J does 8 laps in 84.48 seconds.
   1 lap takes ☐ seconds.

10. Car K does 7 laps in 83.58 seconds.
    1 lap takes ☐ seconds.

Today I scored ☐ out of 10.

Week 11 — Day 3

How many miles have the whales travelled in total?

Whale 1	34 miles
Whale 2	40 kilometres

59 miles

1.
Whale 1	21 miles
Whale 2	16 kilometres

_____ miles

2.
Whale 1	17 miles
Whale 2	24 kilometres

_____ miles

3.
Whale 1	62 miles
Whale 2	48 kilometres

_____ miles

4.
Whale 1	47 miles
Whale 2	80 kilometres

_____ miles

5.
Whale 1	74 miles
Whale 2	32 kilometres

_____ miles

6.
Whale 1	29 miles
Whale 2	88 kilometres

_____ miles

7.
Whale 1	55 miles
Whale 2	64 kilometres

_____ miles

8.
Whale 1	40 miles
Whale 2	56 kilometres

_____ miles

9.
Whale 1	24 miles
Whale 2	72 kilometres

_____ miles

10.
Whale 1	16 miles
Whale 2	96 kilometres

_____ miles

Today I scored _____ out of 10.

Week 11 — Day 4

Use the formula to find the answer.

$y = \dfrac{x + 2}{4}$

When $x = 18$, $y =$ 5

1) $y = 5x + 2$

When $x = 8$, $y =$ ☐

2) $y = 4x + 4$

When $x = 12$, $y =$ ☐

3) $y = \dfrac{x}{3} - 7$

When $x = 36$, $y =$ ☐

4) $y = \dfrac{x + 9}{2}$

When $x = 21$, $y =$ ☐

5) $y = 8x - 11$

When $x =$ ☐, $y = 21$

6) $y = 7x + 5$

When $x =$ ☐, $y = 26$

7) $y = 6x - 9$

When $x =$ ☐, $y = 57$

8) $y = \dfrac{x + 6}{12}$

When $x = 66$, $y =$ ☐

9) $y = \dfrac{x + 8}{5}$

When $x =$ ☐, $y = 3$

10) $y = \dfrac{x}{7} + 11$

When $x =$ ☐, $y = 20$

Today I scored ☐ out of 10.

Week 11 — Day 5

How much money is left? Give your answer to the nearest £1000.

Ben has £12 730. He spends £540 a month for 7 months.

£ 9000 is left.

1. Zane has £11 860. He spends £350 a month for 8 months.
   £ _____ is left.

2. Kim has £9 340. She spends £320 a month for 6 months.
   £ _____ is left.

3. Aled has £6 590. He spends £130 a month for 11 months.
   £ _____ is left.

4. Rose has £13 820. She spends £540 a month for 9 months.
   £ _____ is left.

5. Neil has £14 980. He spends £610 a month for 12 months.
   £ _____ is left.

6. Elle has £17 270. She spends £650 a month for 18 months.
   £ _____ is left.

7. Troy has £14 660. He spends £540 a month for 15 months.
   £ _____ is left.

8. Faye has £12 010. She spends £370 a month for 16 months.
   £ _____ is left.

Today I scored _____ out of 8.

Week 12 — Day 1

Draw the shape on the grid after it has been translated as described.

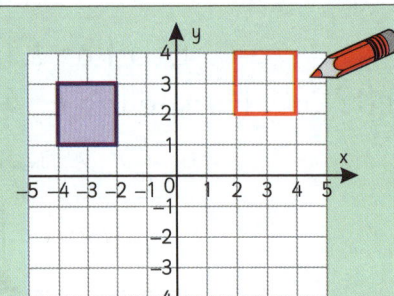

+6 units horizontally, +1 unit vertically

1) +2 units horizontally, +2 units vertically

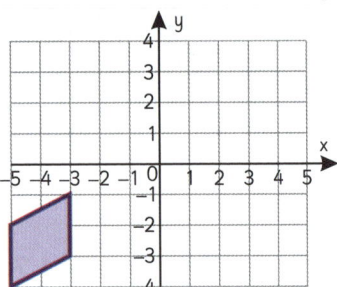

4) +7 units horizontally, −1 units vertically

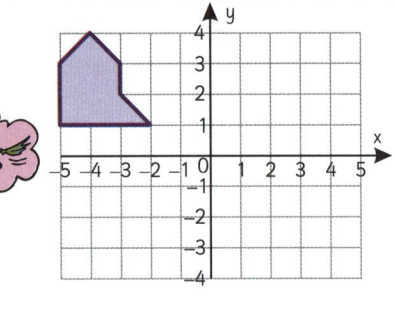

2) +1 units horizontally, −4 units vertically

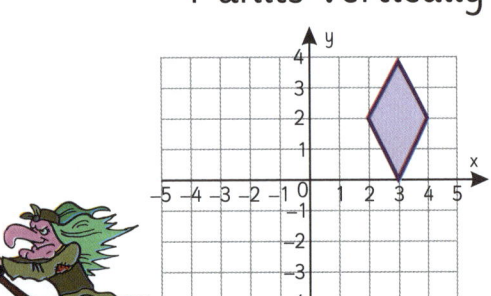

5) −5 units horizontally, +3 units vertically

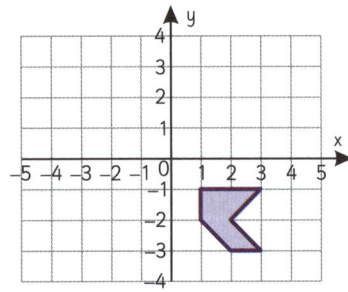

3) −6 units horizontally, +5 units vertically

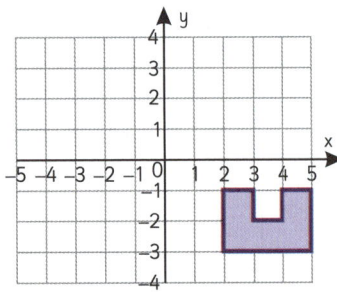

6) −3 units horizontally, +2 units vertically

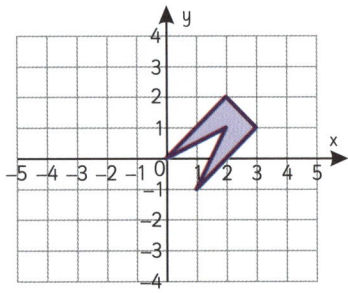

Today I scored ☐ out of 6.

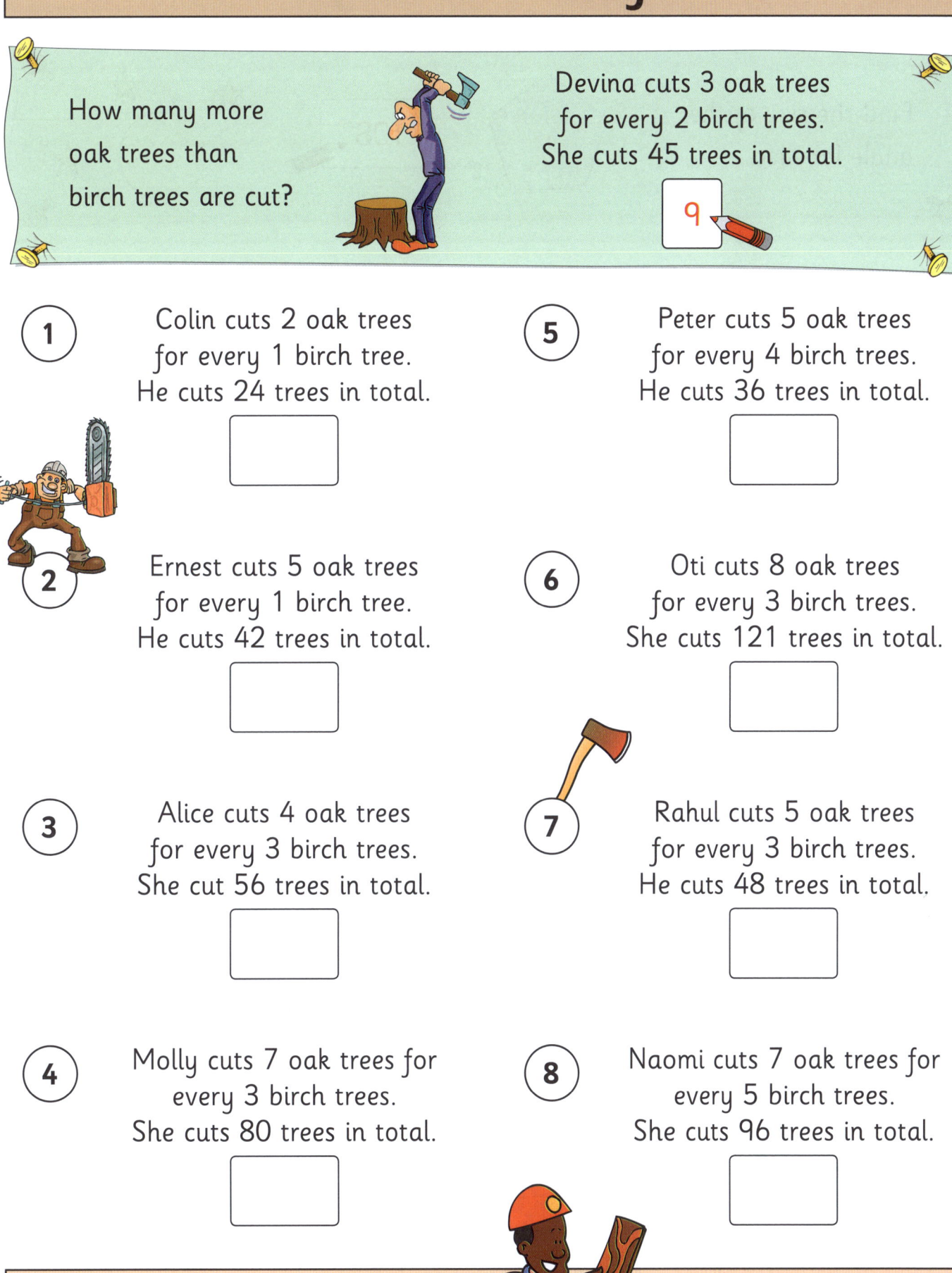

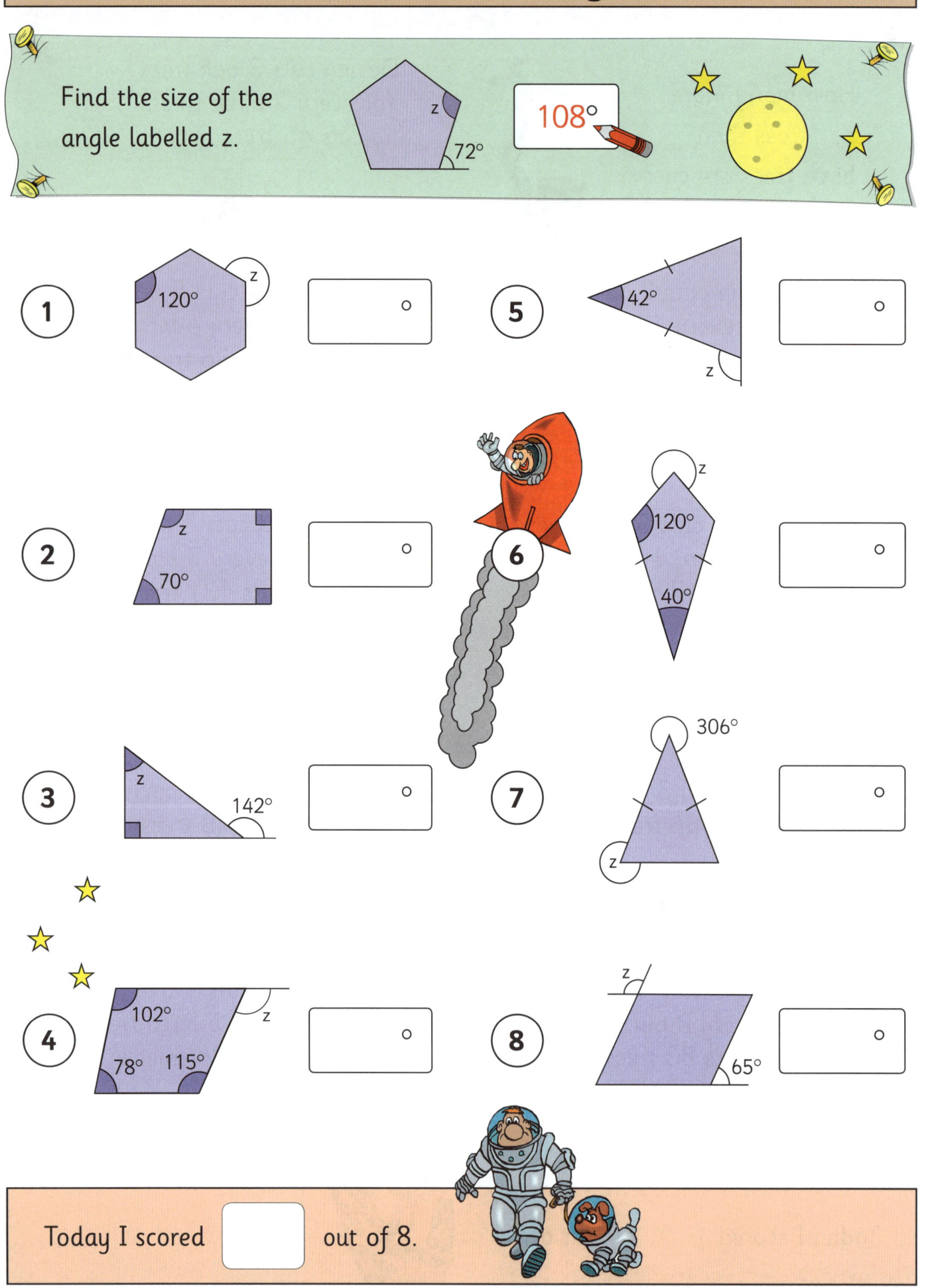

Week 12 — Day 4

Write a word formula for working out the number of vegetables needed for a meal. Use this formula to work out how many vegetables are needed for the number of people given.

For peppers, you halve the number of people and add 5.

peppers = (people ÷ 2) + 5

6 people need 8 peppers.

1. For carrots, you double the number of people and add 4.

   7 people need ___ carrots.

2. For leeks, you halve the number of people and take away 2.

   12 people need ___ leeks.

3. For sprouts, you triple the number of people and add 4.

   8 people need ___ sprouts.

4. For onions, you halve the number of people and add 3.

   18 people need ___ onions.

5. For parsnips, you double the number of people and take away 7.

   11 people need ___ parsnips.

6. For potatoes, you triple the number of people and add 6.

   15 people need ___ potatoes.

Today I scored ___ out of 6.

Week 12 — Day 5

Use the information given to work out the length of the last block.

Carl has five blocks. They have a mean length of 18 cm. Three of the blocks are 15 cm long, and one of the blocks is 23 cm long. How long is the fifth block?

22 cm

1. Mel has four blocks. They have a mean length of 22 cm. Two of the blocks are 21 cm long, and one of the blocks is 26 cm long. How long is the fourth block? ☐ cm

2. Angus has five blocks. They have a mean length of 27 cm. Two of the blocks are 25 cm long, and two of the blocks are 32 cm long. How long is the fifth block? ☐ cm

3. Lele has six blocks. They have a mean length of 19 cm. Three of the blocks are 17 cm long, and two of the blocks are 20 cm long. How long is the sixth block? ☐ cm

4. Joe has seven blocks. They have a mean length of 16 cm. Three of the blocks are 13 cm long, and three of the blocks are 18 cm long. How long is the seventh block? ☐ cm

5. Jez has seven blocks. They have a mean length of 28 cm. Two of the blocks are 25 cm long, and four of the blocks are 29 cm long. How long is the seventh block? ☐ cm

Today I scored ☐ out of 5.

Answers

Week 1 — Day 1

1. (1, 1)
2. (1, 2)
3. (–1, 1)
4. (2, 2)
5. (–2, 2)
6. (–2, 0)
7. (–3, –2)
8. (1, –2)

Week 1 — Day 2

1.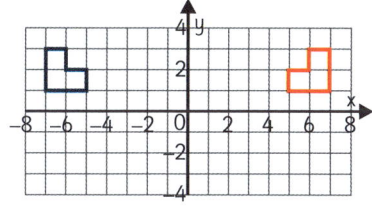
2.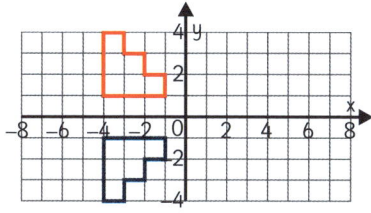
3.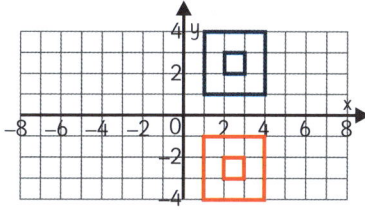
4.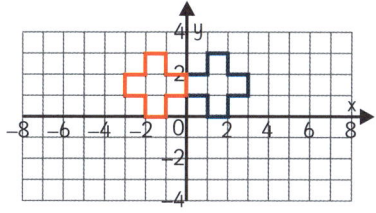
5.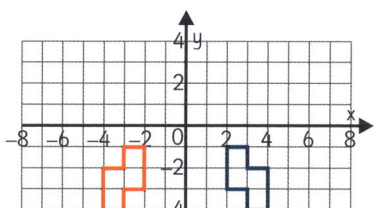
6.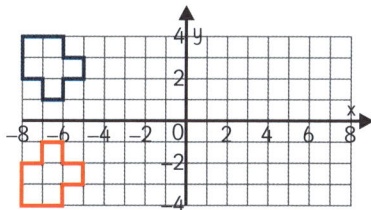
7.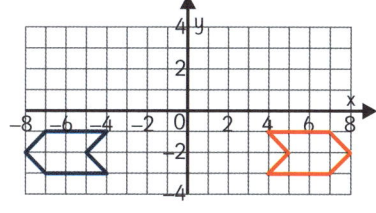
8.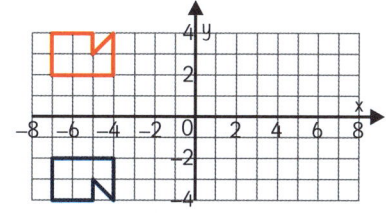

Week 1 — Day 3

1. 96 m³
2. 3000 m³
3. 162 m³
4. 385 m³
5. 384 m³
6. 648 m³
7. 1500 m³
8. 576 m³

Week 1 — Day 4

1. +4 units horizontally, +2 units vertically
2. –6 units horizontally, 0 units vertically
3. –8 units horizontally, +2 units vertically
4. +10 units horizontally, –4 units vertically
5. –11 units horizontally, –5 units vertically

Week 1 — Day 5

1. Socks
2. Swimsuit
3. Racket
4. Shorts
5. Balls
6. Skis
7. Bike
8. Club
9. Gloves
10. Shin pads

Week 2 — Day 1

1. E.g. (500 000 – 100 000) × 3
2. E.g. (7 + 4) × 20 000
3. E.g. (8000 + 4000) ÷ 4
4. E.g. 900 000 × (6 + 3)
5. E.g. (200 000 + 500 000) × 9
6. E.g. (600 000 + 900 000) ÷ 5
7. E.g. 2 × (300 000 + 600 000)
8. E.g. (400 000 – 200 000) ÷ 2
9. E.g. 700 000 ÷ (8 – 1)
10. E.g. 6 × (800 000 – 100 000)

Week 2 — Day 2

1. 7
2. 9
3. 5
4. 12
5. 8
6. 9
7. 11
8. 9
9. 12
10. 11

Week 2 — Day 3

1. 48 000 m²
2. 150 000 m²
3. 70 000 m²
4. 216 000 m²
5. 156 000 m²
6. 231 000 m²
7. 204 000 m²
8. 356 000 m²

Week 2 — Day 4

1.
2.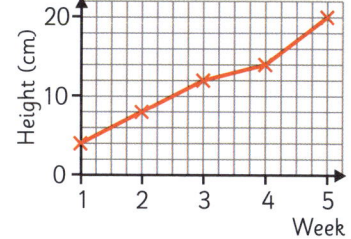
3.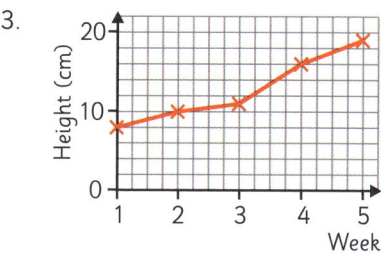
4.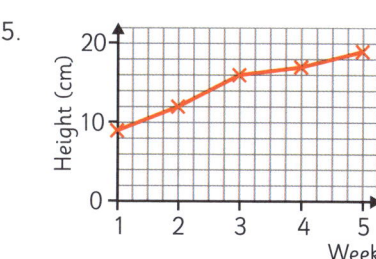
5.
6.

© CGP — Not to be photocopied

Week 2 — Day 5
1. 6 °C
2. 4 °C
3. 5 °C
4. 7 °C
5. 8 °C
6. 6 °C

Week 3 — Day 1
1. $\frac{1}{24}$
2. $\frac{3}{50}$
3. $\frac{3}{28}$
4. $\frac{1}{40}$
5. $\frac{1}{16}$
6. $\frac{1}{12}$
7. $\frac{1}{9}$
8. $\frac{4}{27}$
9. $\frac{3}{22}$
10. $\frac{1}{14}$
11. $\frac{1}{24}$
12. $\frac{1}{14}$

Week 3 — Day 2
1. E.g.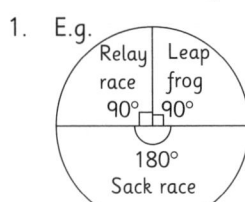
2. E.g.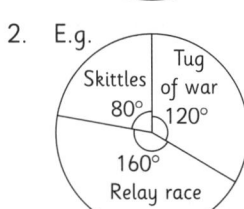
3. E.g.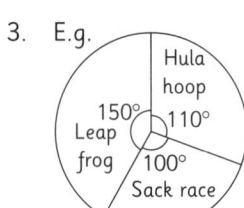
4. E.g.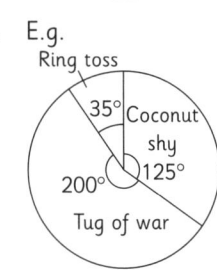

Week 3 — Day 3
1. 8.67 kg
2. 4.28 kg
3. 11.021 kg
4. 299.591 kg
5. 6.092 kg
6. 5.095 kg
7. 16.424 kg
8. 1.05 kg

Week 3 — Day 4
1. 9%
2. 39%
3. 40%
4. 18%
5. 1%
6. 17%
7. 3%
8. 4%

Week 3 — Day 5
1. 18
2. 7
3. 14
4. 4
5. 7
6. 3

Week 4 — Day 1
1. (1, 2)
2. (2, 3)
3. (3, −3)
4. (−2, 3)
5. (−2, −1)
6. (−5, −3)

Week 4 — Day 2
1. $\frac{5}{12}$
2. $\frac{3}{28}$
3. $\frac{14}{25}$
4. $\frac{5}{12}$
5. $\frac{21}{40}$
6. $\frac{5}{11}$
7. $\frac{9}{28}$
8. $\frac{10}{27}$

Week 4 — Day 3
1. 130 minutes
2. 85 minutes
3. 162 minutes
4. 141 minutes
5. 70 minutes
6. 118 minutes
7. 133 minutes
8. 124 minutes

Week 4 — Day 4
1. $\frac{1}{3}$
2. $\frac{2}{5}$
3. $\frac{1}{6}$
4. $\frac{1}{2}$
5. $\frac{3}{4}$
6. $\frac{1}{2}$
7. $\frac{7}{8}$
8. $\frac{4}{5}$
9. $\frac{2}{3}$
10. $\frac{3}{7}$

Week 4 — Day 5
1. 112 m²
2. 90 m²
3. 600 m²
4. 450 m²
5. 288 m²
6. 864 m²
7. 1344 m²
8. 1568 m²

Week 5 — Day 1
1. 300
2. 70 000
3. 400 000
4. 10
5. 8 000 000
6. 900 000
7. 600
8. 1 000 000
9. 50 000
10. 4000
11. 200 000
12. 70 000

Week 5 — Day 2
1. 2.4 kg
2. 6.45 kg
3. 5760 g
4. 810 g
5. 7.684 kg
6. 466 g
7. 8061 g
8. 9073 g
9. 0.846 kg
10. 55 g
11. 0.023 kg
12. 0.007 kg

Week 5 — Day 3
1. E.g.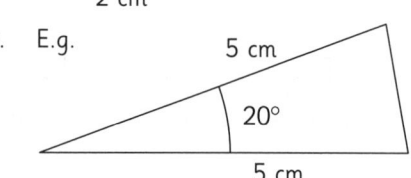
2. E.g.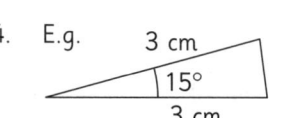
3. E.g.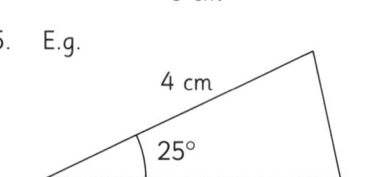
4. E.g.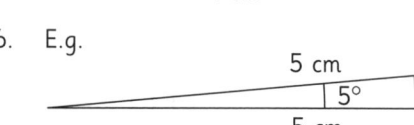
5. E.g.
6. E.g.

Week 5 — Day 4
1. 1600 m
2. 2400 m
3. 2700 m
4. 900 m
5. 3150 m
6. 5850 m
7. 220 m
8. 1700 m
9. 3840 m
10. 7110 m

Week 5 — Day 5
1. 6
2. 2
3. 3
4. 14
5. 16
6. 7
7. 13
8. 4

Week 6 — Day 1
1. 50%
2. 38%
3. 40%
4. 36%
5. 40%
6. 60%
7. 70%
8. 68%

Week 6 — Day 2
1. 6
2. 8
3. 7
4. 6
5. 11
6. 12
7. 13
8. 14
9. 7
10. 8

Week 6 — Day 3

1. 29
2. 67
3. 44
4. 55
5. 67
6. 65
7. 385
8. 888
9. 102
10. 92
11. 110
12. 69

Week 6 — Day 4

1. 3.84 km
2. 5.76 km
3. 1.319 km
4. 5.839 km
5. 4.512 km
6. 5.723 km
7. 6.096 km
8. 7.951 km
9. 12.914 km
10. 3.983 km

Week 6 — Day 5

1. 6 ÷ 19
2. 12 ÷ 13
3. 9 ÷ 12
4. 6 ÷ 15
5. 4 ÷ 21
6. 17 ÷ 9
7. 7 ÷ 3
8. 17 ÷ 6

Week 7 — Day 1

1. 4.89 kg
2. 2.899 kg
3. 7.918 kg
4. 5.195 kg
5. 4.297 kg
6. 7.354 kg
7. 5.093 kg
8. 3.521 kg
9. 5.456 kg
10. 6.024 kg

Week 7 — Day 2

1. 16 km
2. 32 km
3. 24 km
4. 48 km
5. 80 km
6. 40 km
7. 56 km
8. 72 km
9. 88 km
10. 96 km

Week 7 — Day 3

1. X = 1, Y = 4
   X = 3, Y = 2
   X = 7, Y = 1
2. X = 1, Y = 3
   X = 3, Y = 2
   X = 9, Y = 1
3. X = 1, Y = 5
   X = 4, Y = 2
   X = 9, Y = 1
4. X = 1, Y = 4
   X = 6, Y = 2
   X = 16, Y = 1
5. X = 1, Y = 5
   X = 3, Y = 3
   X = 13, Y = 1
6. X = 2, Y = 3
   X = 6, Y = 2
   X = 18, Y = 1

Week 7 — Day 4

1. 100
2. 140
3. 160
4. 90
5. 210
6. 200
7. 280
8. 140
9. 450
10. 360
11. 300
12. 350

Week 7 — Day 5

1. 4 cm
2. 8 cm
3. 12 cm
4. 11 cm
5. 12 cm
6. 18 cm

Week 8 — Day 1

1. Two hundred and thirty four thousand, eight hundred and seventy five
2. One hundred and thirty two thousand and eleven
3. Nine hundred and eight thousand, seven hundred and sixty six
4. Two million, three hundred and forty four thousand, seven hundred and eighty one
5. Four million, five hundred and sixty seven thousand, eight hundred and ninety
6. Seven million, sixty seven thousand, eight hundred and two
7. Six million, eight thousand and forty one

Week 8 — Day 2

1. 4
2. 7
3. 15
4. 35
5. 24
6. 49

Week 8 — Day 3

1. 21 cm²
2. 80 cm²
3. 45 cm²
4. 16 cm²
5. 108 cm²
6. 66 cm²

Week 8 — Day 4

1. 13
2. 4
3. 20
4. 3
5. 3
6. 11

Week 8 — Day 5

1. 118
2. 132
3. 123
4. 203
5. 223
6. 143

Week 9 — Day 1

1. 30 °C
2. 40 °C
3. 46 °C
4. 46 °C
5. 43 °C
6. 49 °C
7. 47 °C
8. 51 °C
9. 41 °C
10. 52 °C

Week 9 — Day 2

1. E.g. (d − 4) × 2 = 4
2. E.g. (c + 7) × 4 = 32
3. E.g. (z × 3) + 5 = 18
4. E.g. (t × 3) ÷ 2 = 6
5. E.g. (x ÷ 4) − 2 = 14
6. E.g. (y × 7) ÷ 6 = 22
7. E.g. (q − 17) ÷ 11 = 1
8. E.g. (m ÷ 9) + 15 = 36

Week 9 — Day 3

1.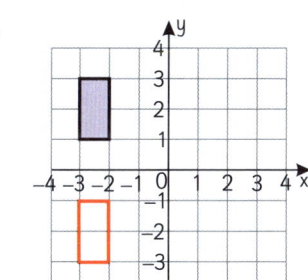
2.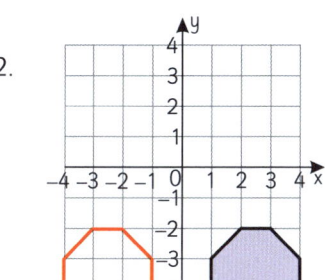
3.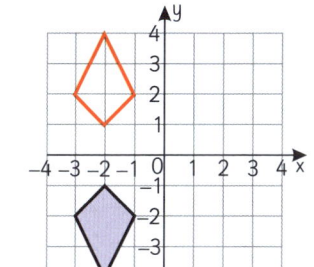
4.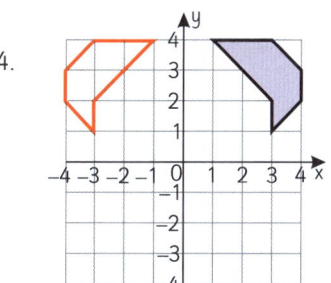
5.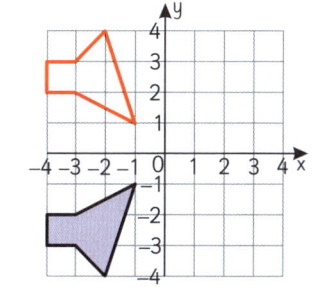

6.

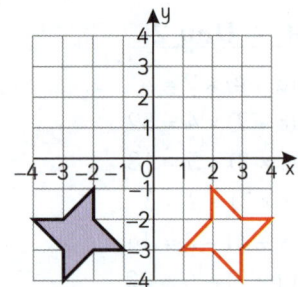

Week 9 — Day 4
1. Natasha   4. Jasmine
2. Summer   5. Adam
3. Claire   6. Chloe

Week 9 — Day 5
1. 2   5. 11
2. 3   6. 11
3. 10   7. 12
4. 4   8. 13

Week 10 — Day 1
1. 3 cm   5. 7 cm
2. 5 cm   6. 6 cm
3. 6 cm   7. 7 cm
4. 4 cm   8. 8 cm

Week 10 — Day 2
1. 720°   5. 3240°
2. 1440°   6. 5040°
3. 540°   7. 2880°
4. 1800°   8. 3960°

Week 10 — Day 3
1. $y = 3x - 3$ 5. $y = x \div 3 + 5$
2. $y = 2 + x$ 6. $y = 2x - 1$
3. $y = x \div 3 + 6$ 7. $y = 2x + 4$
4. $y = 2x + 6$ 8. $y = 2x \div 3$

Week 10 — Day 4
1. 160 cm   5. 40 cm
2. 180 cm   6. 290 cm
3. 25 cm   7. 220 cm
4. 250 cm   8. 30 cm

Week 10 — Day 5
1. 2032 g   5. 2704 g
2. 3020 g   6. 4314 g
3. 3781 g   7. 4768 g
4. 2888 g   8. 4472 g

Week 11 — Day 1
1. 35 m²   6. 35 m²
2. 18 m²   7. 20 m²
3. 8 m²   8. 28 m²
4. 51 m²   9. 70 m²
5. 18 m²   10. 42 m²

Week 11 — Day 2
1. 11.26 seconds
2. 7.95 seconds
3. 8.75 seconds
4. 10.65 seconds
5. 13.68 seconds
6. 12.85 seconds
7. 10.27 seconds
8. 17.15 seconds
9. 10.56 seconds
10. 11.94 seconds

Week 11 — Day 3
1. 31 miles   6. 84 miles
2. 32 miles   7. 95 miles
3. 92 miles   8. 75 miles
4. 97 miles   9. 69 miles
5. 94 miles   10. 76 miles

Week 11 — Day 4
1. 42   6. 3
2. 52   7. 11
3. 5   8. 6
4. 15   9. 7
5. 4   10. 63

Week 11 — Day 5
1. £9000   5. £8000
2. £7000   6. £6000
3. £5000   7. £7000
4. £9000   8. £6000

Week 12 — Day 1
1.

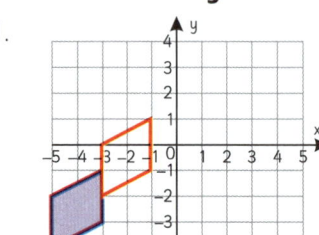

2.

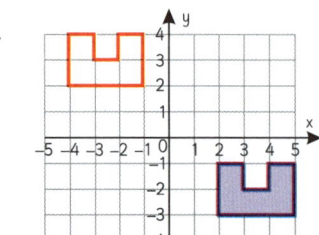

3.

4.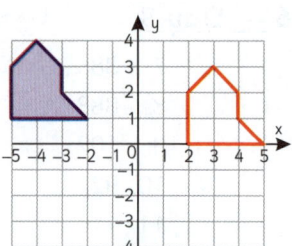

5.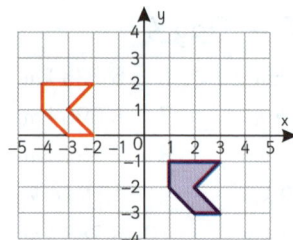

6.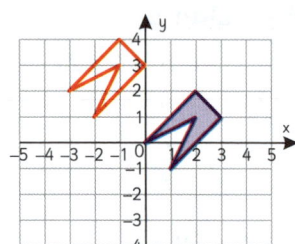

Week 12 — Day 2
1. 8   5. 4
2. 28   6. 55
3. 8   7. 12
4. 32   8. 16

Week 12 — Day 3
1. 240°   5. 111°
2. 110°   6. 280°
3. 52°   7. 297°
4. 115°   8. 115°

Week 12 — Day 4
1. carrots = (people × 2) + 4
   7 people need **18** carrots.
2. leeks = (people ÷ 2) − 2
   12 people need **4** leeks.
3. sprouts = (people × 3) + 4
   8 people need **28** sprouts.
4. onions = (people ÷ 2) + 3
   18 people need **12** onions.
5. parsnips = (people × 2) − 7
   11 people need **15** parsnips.
6. potatoes = (people × 3) + 6
   15 people need **51** potatoes.

Week 12 — Day 5
1. 20 cm
2. 21 cm
3. 23 cm
4. 19 cm
5. 30 cm